OPPOSING
VIEWPOINTS®
SERIES

| Marriage

Other Books of Related Interest

Opposing Viewpoints Series

America's Changing Demographics
Feminism
Gender in the 21st Century
Identity Politics
Toxic Masculinity

At Issue Series

Gender Politics
Male Privilege
Reproductive Rights
The Right to a Living Wage
The Role of Religion in Public Policy

Current Controversies Series

Are There Two Americas?
LGBTQ Rights
Microaggressions, Safe Spaces, and Trigger Warnings
The Political Elite and Special Interests
Universal Health Care

> "Congress shall make no law … abridging the freedom of speech, or of the press."

First Amendment to the US Constitution

The basic foundation of our democracy is the First Amendment guarantee of freedom of expression. The Opposing Viewpoints series is dedicated to the concept of this basic freedom and the idea that it is more important to practice it than to enshrine it.

OPPOSING VIEWPOINTS® SERIES

| Marriage

Lita Sorensen, Book Editor

GREENHAVEN PUBLISHING

#1232013818

Dedicated to James and Loretta Sorensen, John and Ada Sorensen, Lucy and Leon Cardini, Ben and Kathleen Dougan, and Gus and Jeanine Harnack

Published in 2022 by Greenhaven Publishing, LLC
353 3rd Avenue, Suite 255, New York, NY 10010

Articles in Greenhaven Publishing anthologies are often edited for length to meet page
requirements. In addition, original titles of these works are changed to clearly present
the main thesis and to explicitly indicate the author's opinion. Every effort is made to
ensure that Greenhaven Publishing accurately reflects the original intent of the authors.
Every effort has been made to trace the owners of the copyrighted material.

Cover image: LifetimeStock/Shutterstock.com

Library of Congress Cataloging-in-Publication Data

Names: Sorensen, Lita, editor.
Title: Marriage / Lita Sorensen, book editor.
Description: First Edition. | New York : Greenhaven Publishing, 2022. |
  Series: Opposing viewpoints | Includes bibliographical references and
  index. | Contents: Marriage | Audience: Ages 15+ | Audience: Grades
  10–12 | Summary: "Anthology of diverse viewpoints exploring how marriage
  fits into our changing society, including issues of same-sex marriage,
  domestic violence, women's equality, children and divorce, the wedding
  industry, and the Unmarried Equality Movement—the movement for single
  people to attain equal rights to married people"— Provided by
  publisher.
Identifiers: LCCN 2021001753 | ISBN 9781534507685 (library binding) | ISBN
  9781534507661 (paperback)
Subjects: LCSH: Marriage—Juvenile literature. | Same-sex
  marriage—Juvenile literature. | Single people—Juvenile literature. |
  Equality before the law—Juvenile literature.
Classification: LCC HQ734 .M357 2022 | DDC 306.81—dc23
LC record available at https://lccn.loc.gov/2021001753

Manufactured in the United States of America

Website: http://greenhavenpublishing.com

Contents

Chapter 1: What Is Marriage?

Chapter 2: Who Gets Married and Why?

Chapter 3: What Are the Issues Surrounding Marriage Today?

Chapter 4: What Is the Future of the Institution of Marriage?

The Importance of Opposing Viewpoints

Perhaps every generation experiences a period in time in which the populace seems especially polarized, starkly divided on the important issues of the day and gravitating toward the far ends of the political spectrum and away from a consensus-facilitating middle ground. The world that today's students are growing up in and that they will soon enter into as active and engaged citizens is deeply fragmented in just this way. Issues relating to terrorism, immigration, women's rights, minority rights, race relations, health care, taxation, wealth and poverty, the environment, policing, military intervention, the proper role of government—in some ways, perennial issues that are freshly and uniquely urgent and vital with each new generation—are currently roiling the world.

If we are to foster a knowledgeable, responsible, active, and engaged citizenry among today's youth, we must provide them with the intellectual, interpretive, and critical-thinking tools and experience necessary to make sense of the world around them and of the all-important debates and arguments that inform it. After all, the outcome of these debates will in large measure determine the future course, prospects, and outcomes of the world and its peoples, particularly its youth. If they are to become successful members of society and productive and informed citizens, students need to learn how to evaluate the strengths and weaknesses of someone else's arguments, how to sift fact from opinion and fallacy, and how to test the relative merits and validity of their own opinions against the known facts and the best possible available information. The landmark series Opposing Viewpoints has been providing students with just such critical-thinking skills and exposure to the debates surrounding society's most urgent contemporary issues for many years, and it continues to serve this essential role with undiminished commitment, care, and rigor.

The key to the series's success in achieving its goal of sharpening students' critical-thinking and analytic skills resides in its title—

Opposing Viewpoints. In every intriguing, compelling, and engaging volume of this series, readers are presented with the widest possible spectrum of distinct viewpoints, expert opinions, and informed argumentation and commentary, supplied by some of today's leading academics, thinkers, analysts, politicians, policy makers, economists, activists, change agents, and advocates. Every opinion and argument anthologized here is presented objectively and accorded respect. There is no editorializing in any introductory text or in the arrangement and order of the pieces. No piece is included as a "straw man," an easy ideological target for cheap point-scoring. As wide and inclusive a range of viewpoints as possible is offered, with no privileging of one particular political ideology or cultural perspective over another. It is left to each individual reader to evaluate the relative merits of each argument—as he or she sees it, and with the use of ever-growing critical-thinking skills—and grapple with his or her own assumptions, beliefs, and perspectives to determine how convincing or successful any given argument is and how the reader's own stance on the issue may be modified or altered in response to it.

This process is facilitated and supported by volume, chapter, and selection introductions that provide readers with the essential context they need to begin engaging with the spotlighted issues, with the debates surrounding them, and with their own perhaps shifting or nascent opinions on them. In addition, guided reading and discussion questions encourage readers to determine the authors' point of view and purpose, interrogate and analyze the various arguments and their rhetoric and structure, evaluate the arguments' strengths and weaknesses, test their claims against available facts and evidence, judge the validity of the reasoning, and bring into clearer, sharper focus the reader's own beliefs and conclusions and how they may differ from or align with those in the collection or those of their classmates.

Research has shown that reading comprehension skills improve dramatically when students are provided with compelling, intriguing, and relevant "discussable" texts. The subject matter of these collections could not be more compelling, intriguing, or urgently relevant to today's students and the world they are poised to inherit. The anthologized articles and the reading and discussion questions that are included with them also provide the basis for stimulating, lively, and passionate classroom debates. Students who are compelled to anticipate objections to their own argument and identify the flaws in those of an opponent read more carefully, think more critically, and steep themselves in relevant context, facts, and information more thoroughly. In short, using discussable text of the kind provided by every single volume in the Opposing Viewpoints series encourages close reading, facilitates reading comprehension, fosters research, strengthens critical thinking, and greatly enlivens and energizes classroom discussion and participation. The entire learning process is deepened, extended, and strengthened.

For all of these reasons, Opposing Viewpoints continues to be exactly the right resource at exactly the right time—when we most need to provide readers with the critical-thinking tools and skills that will not only serve them well in school but also in their careers and their daily lives as decision-making family members, community members, and citizens. This series encourages respectful engagement with and analysis of opposing viewpoints and fosters a resulting increase in the strength and rigor of one's own opinions and stances. As such, it helps make readers "future ready," and that readiness will pay rich dividends for the readers themselves, for the citizenry, for our society, and for the world at large.

Introduction

> "Marriage responds to the universal fear that a lonely person might call out only to find no one there. It offers the hope of companionship and understanding and assurance that while both still live there will be someone to care for the other."
>
> —Justice Anthony Kennedy in his majority opinion in Obergefell v. Hodges

> "Speculation about whether or not marriage is obsolete overlooks a more important question: What is lost by making marriage the most central relationship in a culture?"
>
> —Mandy Len Catron, "What You Lose When You Gain a Spouse," The Atlantic, July 2, 2019

Marriage can be defined as a consensual union between individuals that is legally and socially sanctioned, enduring, and often based on a sexual relationship of some kind. It is considered by sociologists and anthropologists to be a cultural universal, predominate in all societies in some aspect or form. The concept of marriage has existed throughout history and traditionally is seen as having a key role in humanity's preservation of morality—and the preservation of civilization itself.

A generally accepted and holistic contractual definition of marriage is that of a formal union with social and legal ramifications between two individuals that unites their lives legally, economically, and emotionally. The marriage contract suggests that a couple has a legal obligation to each other from the time they marry throughout their lives or until they decide to divorce. The marriage contract also offers legitimacy to a sexual relationship between the partners and legally recognizes any offspring produced.

Of course, societies are not monocultural, and much diversity exists throughout the world and throughout history via forms of marriage. The concept of marriage in modern Western countries has begun to shift, particularly in regard to divorce and the status of procreation within the marriage union.

In 2001, the first legal acknowledgment of same-sex marriage came when the Netherlands started to recognize same-sex marriages as valid. Throughout the following decades, many additional countries also passed similar legislation: Canada in 2005, France in 2013, the United States in 2015, and Germany in 2017. Additionally, various countries extended the benefits married people usually have to same-sex couples via a registered partnership or civil union.

Only relatively recently has marriage been considered a matter of free choice. Historically, even in Western cultures, romantic love and affection was a secondary concern, and a marriage partner was often carefully chosen by one's family or someone else. In a society where arranged marriage was enacted, a nearly universal custom of engaging a matchmaker was employed. The matchmaker's only responsibility was to broker a marriage that would be acceptable to both the bride's and bridegroom's families. In societies that used matchmakers, some kind of dowry or bride wealth was almost always promised the family of the groom.

By contrast, in societies where marriage partners choose their own mates, dating is the usual way individuals choose partners. Dating is followed by courtship and betrothal, which can be formal or informal, depending on the historical period and cultural specifics within a society.

Sociologists mainly are interested in the idea of marriage because the institution of marriage is historically interconnected with another of humanity's recognized institutions, that of the family. The family can be seen as the most basic unit upon which culture and societies are built. Both of these institutions confer status upon individuals that are socially sanctioned. Questions surrounding what constitutes a family are a source of debate in both politics and religion. Those with conservative values often define family in terms of structure and roles. Religion, another institution within most human societies, also recognizes defining characteristics for marriages that are of a conservative or traditionalist nature in many societies.

The idea of marriage, though sanctioned and respected in most societies, is not without its controversies. Issues such as child brides, polygamy, forced unions, and the relatively new idea that marriage itself is unfair to single people in a variety of ways, but especially legally and financially, can become controversial as modern cultures forge new definitions of marriage for themselves.

One large subject of contention is the rights of women within the traditional concept of marriage. Historically speaking, wives had few rights within the marriage contract and were considered the property of their husbands. Wives could not own property of their own and had little legal power in most Western cultures. Gradually, since the late 1800s, marriage has undergone a redefinition, improving the rights of women within the marriage contract.

Equally, the role of violence against women, once deemed a "right" of husbands over wives, has been scrutinized by modern societies, as the definition of human rights began to form in the late twentieth century.

Child marriage and forced marriage also have come under fire as issues of international law, as modern society recognizes the rights of individuals to consent to enter into matrimony and have the legal right to divorce. In some countries, even to this day, it is still very difficult for partners to obtain the right to divorce, especially for women.

Even as same-sex partner marriages have gained support in modern cultures, the legal and social rights of single people who do not marry has come to the forefront in recent years. Proponents of single people's rights note that single people suffer financially and socially and are often stigmatized because of their lack of a marriage contract. They point out how this does not support the aims of human rights initiatives.

As modern society refocuses views on that most intimate of partnerships, marriage, understanding perspectives originating from a variety of viewpoints becomes increasingly important. In chapters titled "What Is Marriage?" "Who Gets Married and Why?" "What Are the Issues Surrounding Marriage Today?" and "What Is the Future of the Institution of Marriage?," *Opposing Viewpoints: Marriage* offers access to outlooks culled from sources that point to critical questions that must be answered surrounding the topic of marriage as society moves forward.

OPPOSING
VIEWPOINTS®
SERIES

CHAPTER 1

What Is Marriage?

Chapter Preface

The definition of the word *marriage* can be traced back to Middle English circa 1300. Its meaning is "action of entering into wedlock" and also the "state or condition of being husband and wife, matrimony, wedlock." Looking even further back into the history of the word, *marriage* is derived from the Latin word *maritatus*, or *maritare*, meaning "to wed, marry, give in marriage."

The word is a very old one, with the institution itself perhaps predating even the language used to categorize it. Most ancient societies needed a system of rules to surround the perpetuation of the species and laws upon which to handle property rights and bloodlines. Hence, the institution of marriage was created. As an example, one law from ancient Hebrew societies required a man to become the husband of his deceased brother's widow.

The main goal of marriage early on in human societies was to produce alliances between families. In *The Power of Myth*, mythologist Joseph Campbell noted that the idea of romantic love only originated in the twelfth century, when it was first mentioned by troubadours. The notion of romance or romantic love did not exist until medieval times. The idea of consent in a marriage may be traced to the Roman Catholic pope Nicholas I, who declared in 866, "If the consent be lacking in a marriage, all other celebrations, even should the union be consummated, are rendered void." In general, the idea of consent has remained important in most religious and legal institutions throughout human history.

The viewpoints in this chapter offer the reader a glimpse into further defining what we mean by this thing we call marriage, the essence of which has changed throughout the centuries and continues to evolve to this day.

"In most societies, a marriage is considered a permanent social and legal contract and relationship between two people that is based on mutual rights and obligations among the spouses."

Marriage Is the Basis for the Institution of the Family

Ashley Crossman

In the following viewpoint, Ashley Crossman offers a broad, modern sociological perspective and definition of what marriage encompasses in today's societies throughout much of the world. The author lists some distinguishing characteristics that most marriages possess and discusses the various types of marriage that have proliferated in world cultures. Ashley Crossman is a sociology writer and holds a PhD from Arizona State University.

As you read, consider the following questions:

1. What is a basic definition of marriage, according to the viewpoint?
2. What other institutions in society sanction marriage?
3. According to the author, what are some characteristics of marriage?

"The Definition of Marriage in Sociology," by Ashley Crossman, Dotdash Publishing Family, November 1, 2019. Reprinted by permission.

Sociologists define marriage as a socially supported union involving two or more individuals in what is regarded as a stable, enduring arrangement typically based at least in part on a sexual bond of some kind.

Overview

Depending on the society, marriage may require religious and/or civil sanction, although some couples may come to be considered married simply by living together for a period of time (common law marriage). Though marriage ceremonies, rules, and roles may differ from one society to another, marriage is considered a cultural universal, which means that it is present as a social institution in all cultures.

Marriage serves several functions. In most societies, it serves to socially identify children by defining kinship ties to a mother, father, and extended relatives. It also serves to regulate sexual behavior, to transfer, preserve, or consolidate property, prestige, and power, and most importantly, it is the basis for the institution of the family.

Social Characteristics of Marriage

In most societies, a marriage is considered a permanent social and legal contract and relationship between two people that is based on mutual rights and obligations among the spouses. A marriage is often based on a romantic relationship, though this is not always the case. But regardless, it typically signals a sexual relationship between two people. A marriage, however, does not simply exist between the married partners, but rather, is codified as a social institution in legal, economic, social, and spiritual/religious ways. Because a marriage is recognized by law and by religious institutions, and involves economic ties between the spouses, a dissolution of marriage (annulment or divorce) must, in turn, involve a dissolution of the marriage relationship in all of these realms.

Typically, the institution of marriage begins with a period of courtship that culminates in an invitation to marry. This is followed by the marriage ceremony, during which mutual rights and responsibilities may be specifically stated and agreed to. In many places, the state or a religious authority must sanction a marriage in order for it to be considered valid and legal.

In many societies, including the Western world and the United States, marriage is widely considered the basis of and foundation for family. This is why a marriage is often greeted socially with immediate expectations that the couple will produce children, and why children that are born outside of marriage are sometimes branded with the stigma of illegitimacy.

The Social Functions of Marriage

Marriage has several social functions that are important within the societies and cultures where the marriage takes place. Most commonly, marriage dictates the roles that spouses play in each other's lives, in the family, and in society at large. Typically these roles involve a division of labor between the spouses, such that each is responsible for different tasks that are necessary within the family.

American sociologist Talcott Parsons wrote on this topic and outlined a theory of roles within a marriage and household, wherein wives/mothers play the expressive role of a caregiver who takes care of socialization and emotional needs of others in the family, while the husband/father is responsible for the task role of earning money to support the family. In keeping with this thinking, a marriage often serves the function of dictating the social status of the spouses and the couple, and of creating a hierarchy of power between the couple. Societies in which the husband/father holds the most power in the marriage are known as patriarchies. Conversely, matriarchal societies are those in which wives/mothers hold the most power.

Marriage also serves the social function of determining family names and lines of familial descent. In the US and much of the

Western world, a common practice is patrilineal descent, meaning the family name follows that of the husband/father. However, many cultures, including some within Europe and many in Central and Latin America, follow matrilineal descent. Today, it is common for newly married couples to create a hyphenated family name that preserves the named lineage of both sides, and for children to bear the surnames of both parents.

Different Types of Marriages

In the Western world, monogamous marriage between two spouses is the most common form of marriage. Other forms of marriage that occur around the world include polygamy (a marriage of more than two spouses), polyandry (a marriage of a wife with more than one husband), and polygyny (the marriage of a husband with more than one wife). (In common usage, polygamy is often misused to refer to polygyny.) As such, the rules of marriage, the division of labor within a marriage, and what constitutes the roles of husbands, wives, and spouses generally are subject to change and are most often negotiated by the partners within the marriage, rather than firmly dictated by tradition.

Expanding the Right to Marry

Over time, the institution of marriage has expanded, and more individuals have won the right to marry. Same-sex marriage is increasingly common and in many places, including the United States, has been sanctioned by law and by many religious groups. In the US, the 2015 Supreme Court decision *Obergefell v. Hodges* struck down laws banning same-sex marriage. This change in practice, law, and cultural norms and expectations for what a marriage is and who can participate in it reflects the fact that marriage itself is a social construct.

> *"The idea of marriage as a sexually exclusive, romantic union between one man and one woman is a relatively recent development."*

Marriage Has Changed over the Centuries
The Week

In the following viewpoint, authors from The Week *offer readers a historical perspective on marriage. The viewpoint also answers frequently asked questions about the role of romance, religion, and types of marriages enacted throughout human history. Some of the facts may surprise you. For instance, same-sex bonds occurred in earlier cultures. The Week is a weekly news publication with editions in the United Kingdom and United States. It was founded in 1995.*

As you read, consider the following questions:

1. What are some characteristics of marriage throughout history?
2. How has love been connected to marriage, according to the viewpoint?
3. How did marriage begin?

"How Marriage Has Changed over Centuries," by *The Week* Staff, The Week Publications Inc., June 1, 2012. Reprinted by permission.

Has marriage always had the same definition? Actually, the institution has been in a process of constant evolution. Pair-bonding began in the Stone Age as a way of organizing and controlling sexual conduct and providing a stable structure for child-rearing and the tasks of daily life.

But that basic concept has taken many forms across different cultures and eras. "Whenever people talk about traditional marriage or traditional families, historians throw up their hands," said Steven Mintz, a history professor at Columbia University. "We say, 'When and where?'" The ancient Hebrews, for instance, engaged in polygamy—according to the Bible, King Solomon had 700 wives and 300 concubines—and men have taken multiple wives in cultures throughout the world, including China, Africa, and among American Mormons in the 19th century. Polygamy is still common across much of the Muslim world.

The idea of marriage as a sexually exclusive, romantic union between one man and one woman is a relatively recent development. Until two centuries ago, said Harvard historian Nancy Cott, "monogamous households were a tiny, tiny portion" of the world population, found in "just Western Europe and little settlements in North America."

When Did People Start Marrying?

The first recorded evidence of marriage contracts and ceremonies dates to 4,000 years ago, in Mesopotamia. In the ancient world, marriage served primarily as a means of preserving power, with kings and other members of the ruling class marrying off daughters to forge alliances, acquire land, and produce legitimate heirs. Even in the lower classes, women had little say over whom they married. The purpose of marriage was the production of heirs, as implied by the Latin word *matrimonium*, which is derived from *mater* (mother).

When Did the Church Get Involved?

In ancient Rome, marriage was a civil affair governed by imperial law. But when the empire collapsed, in the 5th century, church courts took over and elevated marriage to a holy union. As the church's power grew through the Middle Ages, so did its influence over marriage. In 1215, marriage was declared one of the church's seven sacraments, alongside rites like baptism and penance. But it was only in the 16th century that the church decreed that weddings be performed in public, by a priest, and before witnesses.

What Role Did Love Play?

For most of human history, almost none at all. Marriage was considered too serious a matter to be based on such a fragile emotion. "If love could grow out of it, that was wonderful," said Stephanie Coontz, author of *Marriage, a History.* "But that was

MARRIAGE AND BRITAIN'S MONARCHY

On April 29, 2011, in London, England, Prince William, Duke of Cambridge, married Catherine Middleton, a commoner. It is rare, though not unheard of, for a member of the British royal family to marry a commoner. Kate Middleton has an upper-class background, but does not have royal ancestry. Her father was a former flight dispatcher and her mother a former flight attendant and owner of Party Pieces. According to Grace Wong's 2011 article titled, "Kate Middleton: A family business that built a princess," "[t]he business grew to the point where [her father] quit his job . . . and it's evolved from a mom-and-pop outfit run out of a shed . . . into a venture operated out of three converted farm buildings in Berkshire." Kate and William met when they were both students at the University of St. Andrews in Scotland (Köhler 2010).

Britain's monarchy arose during the Middle Ages. Its social hierarchy placed royalty at the top and commoners on the bottom. This was generally a closed system, with people born into positions of nobility. Wealth was passed from generation to generation through primogeniture, a law stating that all property would be inherited by gravy." In fact, love and marriage were once widely regarded as incompatible with one another. A Roman politician was expelled from the Senate in the 2nd century B.C. for kissing his wife in public—behavior the essayist Plutarch condemned as "disgraceful." In the 12th and 13th centuries, the European aristocracy viewed extramarital affairs as the highest form of romance, untainted by the gritty realities of daily life. And as late as the 18th century, the French philosopher Montesquieu wrote that any man who was in love with his wife was probably too dull to be loved by another woman.

When Did Romance Enter the Picture?

In the 17th and 18th centuries, when Enlightenment thinkers pioneered the idea that life was about the pursuit of happiness. They advocated marrying for love rather than wealth or status.

the firstborn son. If the family had no son, the land went to the next closest male relation. Women could not inherit property, and their social standing was primarily determined through marriage.

The arrival of the Industrial Revolution changed Britain's social structure. Commoners moved to cities, got jobs, and made better livings. Gradually, people found new opportunities to increase their wealth and power. Today, the government is a constitutional monarchy with the prime minister and other ministers elected to their positions, and with the royal family's role being largely ceremonial. The long-ago differences between nobility and commoners have blurred, and the modern class system in Britain is similar to that of the United States (McKee 1996).

Today, the royal family still commands wealth, power, and a great deal of attention. When Queen Elizabeth II retires or passes away, Prince Charles will be first in line to ascend the throne. If he abdicates (chooses not to become king) or dies, the position will go to Prince William. If that happens, Kate Middleton will be called Queen Catherine and hold the position of queen consort. She will be one of the few queens in history to have earned a college degree (Marquand 2011).

"What Is Social Stratification?" by Lumen Learning

This trend was augmented by the Industrial Revolution and the growth of the middle class in the 19th century, which enabled young men to select a spouse and pay for a wedding, regardless of parental approval. As people took more control of their love lives, they began to demand the right to end unhappy unions. Divorce became much more commonplace.

Did Marriage Change in the 20th Century?

Dramatically. For thousands of years, law and custom enforced the subordination of wives to husbands. But as the women's-rights movement gained strength in the late 19th and 20th centuries, wives slowly began to insist on being regarded as their husbands' equals, rather than their property. "By 1970," said Marilyn Yalom, author of *A History of the Wife*, "marriage law had become gender-neutral in Western democracy." At the same time, the rise of effective contraception fundamentally transformed marriage: Couples could choose how many children to have, and even to have no children at all. If they were unhappy with each other, they could divorce—and nearly half of all couples did. Marriage had become primarily a personal contract between two equals seeking love, stability, and happiness. This new definition opened the door to gays and lesbians claiming a right to be married, too. "We now fit under the Western philosophy of marriage," said E.J. Graff, a lesbian and the author of *What Is Marriage For?* In one very real sense, Coontz says, opponents of gay marriage are correct when they say traditional marriage has been undermined. "But, for better and for worse, traditional marriage has already been destroyed," she says, "and the process began long before anyone even dreamed of legalizing same-sex marriage."

Gay "Marriage" in Medieval Europe

Same-sex unions aren't a recent invention. Until the 13th century, male-bonding ceremonies were common in churches across the Mediterranean. Apart from the couples' gender, these events were almost indistinguishable from other marriages of the era.

Twelfth-century liturgies for same-sex unions—also known as "spiritual brotherhoods"—included the recital of marriage prayers, the joining of hands at the altar, and a ceremonial kiss. Some historians believe these unions were merely a way to seal alliances and business deals. But Eric Berkowitz, author of *Sex and Punishment*, says it is "difficult to believe that these rituals did not contemplate erotic contact. In fact, it was the sex between the men involved that later caused same-sex unions to be banned." That happened in 1306, when the Byzantine Emperor Andronicus II declared such ceremonies, along with sorcery and incest, to be unchristian.

> *"Child marriage is often referred to as 'early' and/or 'forced' marriage since children, given their age, are not able to give free, prior and informed consent."*

Child Marriage Is a Practice from the Past That Must End

United Nations Population Fund

In the following excerpted viewpoint, the United Nations Population Fund argues that child marriage is a human rights violation. Although child marriage was a practice sanctioned by many cultures in the past, when examined from a modern-day legal and human rights perspective, it is clear that it should be put to an end. The authors cite patriarchal societies and the roles between men and women as causative factors reinforcing the practice. The United Nations Population Fund is the United Nations' sexual and reproductive health agency. Its goal is to deliver a world where every pregnancy is by choice, pregnancies are wanted, and every person's life potential is fulfilled.

"Marrying Too Young: End Child Marriage," United Nations Population Fund, January 2020. Reprinted by permission.

As you read, consider the following questions:

1. According to the viewpoint, why is child marriage a human rights violation?
2. What is consent in marriage?
3. Why is child marriage dangerous, according to the author?

Child marriage occurs when one or both of the spouses are below the age of 18. Child marriage is a violation of Article 16(2) of the Universal Declaration of Human Rights, which states that "marriage shall be entered into only with the free and full consent of the intending spouses." Article 16 of the Convention on the Elimination of All Forms of Discrimination Against Women (CEDAW) states that women should have the same right as men to "freely choose a spouse and to enter into marriage only with their free and full consent," and that the "betrothal and marriage of a child shall have no legal effect."[2]

The Convention on the Rights of the Child (CRC) sets out the human rights of children: the right to survive; the right to develop to their fullest; the right to protection from harmful practices, abuse and exploitation; and the right to participate fully in family, cultural and social life. In signing the convention, governments also committed to take "all effective and appropriate measures with a view to abolish traditional practices prejudicial to the health of the children,"[3] which includes, among other practices, female genital mutilation/cutting and child marriage.

Any departure from the obligations enshrined in these conventions is a violation of human rights. By becoming party to these conventions, governments agree to hold themselves accountable for violations.

In a landmark international consensus, the Programme of Action adopted by the International Conference on Population and Development (ICPD) in 1994, countries agreed on measures to eliminate child marriage[4] as well as to "strictly enforce laws to ensure that marriage is entered into only with the free and full consent of the intending spouses."[5]

[...]

Devastating—Even Life-Threatening—Consequences

The term "child marriage" is used to describe a legal or customary union between two people, of whom one or both spouses is below the age of 18.[6] While boys can be subjected to child marriage, the practice affects girls in greater numbers and with graver consequences. Child marriage is often referred to as "early" and/ or "forced" marriage since children, given their age, are not able to give free, prior and informed consent to their marriage partners or to the timing of their marriage. Many girls, for example, may have little understanding of or exposure to other life options. They may "willingly" accept marriage as their allotted fate. An element of coercion may also be involved if families apply social or emotional pressure or urge marriage for economic reasons, or further advocate marriage in the (misguided) belief that such a union will keep their daughters safe.

Yet, for millions of girls, marriage is anything but safe and anything but consistent with their best interests. Child marriage violates girls' rights and it does so in a number of ways. It effectively brings a girl's childhood and adolescence to a premature and unnatural end by imposing adult roles and responsibilities before she is physically, psychologically and emotionally prepared. It is not uncommon for marriage to impose social isolation on girls bringing unwanted separation from their friends and family. Often child marriage brings an end to a girl's chance of continued education.[7] Girls may be removed from school for many reasons: recent research suggests that dropping out of school is less likely to be a direct consequence of child marriage than of poverty, the low status afforded to women, and social norms that lead parents to discount the value of investing in girls and their education.

But under these conditions, when girls drop out of school, they become even more vulnerable to child marriage.[8]

Once married, girls are likely to feel, and in many cases are, powerless to refuse sex. They are likely to find it difficult to insist on condom use by their husbands, who commonly are older and more sexually experienced, making the girls especially vulnerable to HIV and other sexually transmitted infections.[9] At its worst, child marriage can be tantamount to bonded labour or enslavement. It can be a sentence to regular exposure to domestic or sexual violence, and a pathway to commercial exploitation.[10]

Married girls are often under pressure to become pregnant immediately or soon after marriage, although they are still children themselves and know little about sex or reproduction. A pregnancy too early in life before a girl's body is fully mature is a major risk to both mother and baby. Complications of pregnancy and childbirth are the main causes of death among adolescent girls ages 15–19 years old in developing countries. Among the disabilities associated with early childbirth is obstetric fistula, an injury which leaves girls in constant pain, vulnerable to infection, incontinent, and often shunned by their husbands, families and communities.

Nearly 16 million teenage girls aged 15–19 years old in developing countries give birth every year. In nine out of ten cases, the mother is already married. Preventing child marriage would significantly help to reduce early pregnancy, and the associated maternal death or disability. At the same time, girls would face a reduced risk of HIV infection.

Beyond the immediate implications, child marriage denies girls the opportunity to fully develop their potential as healthy, productive and empowered citizens. Child marriage robs girls of their girlhood, entrenching them and their future families in poverty, limiting their life choices, and generating high development costs for communities.

The Legal, Social and Cultural Dimensions

A recent analysis of the world's marriage patterns showed that although child marriage persists, the minimum legal age for marriage without parental consent is 18 years in most countries.[11] Families and girls themselves may simply not know that laws against child marriage exist, and enforcement of such laws is often lax. Laws also vary widely, and exceptions are made on different grounds, most commonly when parents or other authorities, such as a judge or community elder, grant their consent.

In 2010, 158 countries reported that 18 years was the minimum legal age for marriage for women without parental consent or approval by a pertinent authority.[12] However, in 146 countries, state or customary law allows girls younger than 18 to marry with the consent of parents or other authorities; in 52 countries, girls under

KISSING COUSINS?

A new study shows that it's okay to have children with first cousins despite being related. The new study shows when people stopped marrying their cousins, and the genetic effects of having children with cousins.

Many famous people have married their cousins.

The paper published in the journal *Science* shows that from 1650 to 1850 people would, on average, marry their fourth cousins. The following century this changed, thanks to technological changes and the growth of cities. By 1950 people were marrying, on average, their seventh cousins.

Transportation played a large role in the change. Improved modes of transportation allowed people to travel further to look for a spouse. Before 1950, people tended to stay within a six-mile radius of where they were born and stayed just in the same place.

Other factors that contributed to the decrease in cousin marriage include changing social norms, shrinking family sizes, and the increasing autonomy of women. Cousin marriage became a taboo after it had been the norm for its usefulness in keeping money in the family.

age 15 can marry with parental consent. In contrast, 18 is the legal age for marriage without consent among males in 180 countries. Additionally, in 105 countries, boys can marry with the consent of a parent or a pertinent authority, and in 23 countries, boys under age 15 can marry with parental consent.[13] The lack of gender equality in the law's treatment of the issue of consent reinforces social norms that dictate it is somehow acceptable for girls to marry earlier than boys. Social norms and customs may further dictate that once a girl is married, she be regarded as a woman, even though she may be barely 12 years old.

Even with the appropriate laws against child marriage in place, the practice persists for a variety of complex, interrelated reasons. Men exercise the preponderance of power in nearly every aspect of life, which restricts women's and girls' exercise of their rights and

---

Shrinking family sizes would have left fewer people to be related to. Family sizes were much larger, increasing the chances of being related to someone else.

After the end of the Civil War, states began to outlaw marriage between cousins.

People who are first cousins share 12.5 percent of their DNA. This drops the further away the relation is to the person. Sharing a number of genes is not good for preventing genetic diseases. Variety in genetics is good for preventing disease.

Research shows that children between first cousins have a 4 to 7 percent chance of being born with birth defects. Those that are more distantly related have a 3 to 4 percent chance of having children born with birth defects.

This would not be a large problem since the chances can be pretty similar. The problem would arise when the next generation of children would have children with their first cousins. Children from those unions would have a lot of genetic material in common, increasing the chance of birth defects.

"Science Says It's Okay to Marry Your Cousin but Not for Your Kids to Marry Theirs," by Jean-Pierre Chigne, *Tech Times*, March 8, 2018.

denies them an equal role in their households and communities. Unequal gender norms put a much higher value on boys and men than on girls and women. When girls from birth lack the same perceived value as boys, families and communities may discount the benefits of educating and investing in their daughters' development.

In addition, girls' perceived value may shift once they reach puberty and their sexuality suddenly looms front and centre. Child marriage is often seen as a safeguard against premarital sex, and the duty to protect the girl from sexual harassment and violence is transferred from father to husband.

Poverty is a major factor underlying child marriage. Many parents genuinely believe that marriage will secure their daughters' futures and that it is in their best interests. Alternatively, girls may be viewed as an economic burden, as a commodity, or a means for settling familial debts or disputes, or securing social, economic or political alliances.[14] Customary requirements such as dowries or bride prices may also enter into families' considerations, especially in communities where families can give a lower dowry for younger brides.[15]

Girls' vulnerability to child marriage can increase during humanitarian crises when family and social structures are disrupted. In times of conflict and natural disaster, parents may marry off their young daughters as a last resort, either to bring the family some income in time of economic hardship, or to offer the girl some sort of protection, particularly in contexts where sexual violence is common. These girls are called "famine brides," for example, in food-insecure Kenya.[16] Young girls were married to "tsunami widowers" in Sri Lanka, Indonesia and India[17] as a way to obtain state subsidies for marrying and starting a family.[18] During the conflicts in Liberia, Uganda and Sudan, girls were abducted and given as "bush wives" to warlords, or even given by their families in exchange for protection.

Social norms and perceptions that tolerate inequity in gender roles and responsibilities must change, Programmes around the world, including those supported by UNFPA, are making headway. Once parents and communities understand the irreparable harm that the practice of child marriage can inflict on girls, practices can shift. Alternatives to child marriage that build up girls' assets, coupled with activities to change harmful social norms, must be introduced and implemented so that girls can enjoy the childhood to which they are entitled, and have the space to grow, learn and be a girl. Just as important is instilling the notion that every person is endowed with inalienable human rights and should be treated with dignity and respect.

Endnotes

2. United Nations Population Fund, and United Nations Children's Fund, 2010, *Women's & Children's Rights: Making the connection*, UNFPA, New York, p. 42.
3. The Convention of the Rights of the Child, Article 24.3. Available at: <www.unicef.org /crc/>. Currently, 193 countries—excluding Somalia, South Sudan and the United States—are party to the Convention.
4. International Conference on Population and Development (ICPD) Programme of Action, para. 5.5. Available at: <www.unfpa.org/public/icpd/>, accessed August 2012.
5. ICPD Programme of Action, para 4.21.
6. Article 1 of the Convention on the Rights of the Child establishes that a child is any human being under the age of 18 unless, under state law, majority is attained earlier.
7. Karei, E.M. and A. Erulker, 2010, *Building Programs to Address Child Marriage: The Berhane Hewan experience in Ethiopia*, Population Council, New York.
8. Karei, EM and A. Erulker 2010.
9. United Nations Population Fund, and United Nations Children's Fund, 2010, *Women's & Children's Rights: Making the connection*, UNFPA, New York, p. 39.
10. UNFPA and UNICEF 2010.
11. United Nations Population Division, Department for Economic and Social Affairs, 2011, *Population Facts No. 2011/1*, UNPD-DESA, New York.
12. UNPD-DESA 2011.
13. UNPD-DESA 2011.
14. Amin, S. (January 2011). "Programs to address child marriage: Framing the Problem." *Promoting Healthy, Safe, and Productive Transitions to Adulthood.* Population Council Brief No. 14.
15. Amin, S. (January 2011).
16. A. North "Drought, drop out and early marriage: Feeling the effects of climate change in East Africa," Equals 24, 4, 2009.
17. R. Krishnamurthy, "Review of Sexual and Reproductive Health Rights in the Context of Disasters in Asia," Asian Pacific Resource and Research Centre for Women (ARROW) Chennai: ARROW, 2009.
18. Plan International, *Breaking Vows: Early and Forced Marriage and Girls' Education*, June 2011, p. 9.

> *"Despite today's popular view that marriage equals love, matrimony is not actually grounded in love or intimacy."*

Marriage Is Historically Based on Patriarchy

Caroline Zielinski

In the following viewpoint, Caroline Zielinski argues that heterosexual marriage is nothing but a historical attempt to reinforce patriarchy and control over women and their offspring and that love often has nothing to do with it. The author relates that marriage has always been based on an unequal partnership. Caroline Zielinski is an Australian-based freelance journalist whose work has appeared in the Guardian, *in the* Sydney Morning Herald, *and for the Australian Broadcasting Corporation.*

As you read, consider the following questions:

1. How, according to the author, does patriarchy order marriage?
2. How are women's bodies controlled through marriage, according to the viewpoint?
3. Why does the author say she will not marry?

"First Comes Love, Then Comes Marriage. Not for Me, Thanks," by Caroline Zielinski, *Daily Telegraph,* April 15, 2015. Reprinted by permission.

Historically, women have always been disadvantaged by the institution of marriage. I am just going to preface this article as talking exclusively about heterosexual marriage. There are not enough words to explore gay marriage, and I couldn't do it justice nor give it the respect it deserves.

The meaning of marriage is so deeply rooted in patriarchy and gender inequality, that, in the modern sense, it does not make sense for a young woman to tie the knot unless she has a partner willing to reject all traditional overtures of marriage.

In the past, women were generally forced into marriage for economic security. In a world where the "welfare state" did not exist, a woman's best chance at survival was to marry, and to marry well. But as soon as she married, the woman's rights, independence and even identity—thus, the Mrs. Dean Jackson title—were surpassed by the will of her husband's, who became her legal guardian in every way.

Despite today's popular view that marriage equals love, matrimony is not actually grounded in love or intimacy: historically, it was a strategic alliance between two families, more often than not orchestrated by the families to ensure long-term stability and prosperity for the maximum amount of people.

If you think about it, marriage is a brilliant invention that, in the past, simultaneously ensured women's rights and feelings remained subservient, and that reproduction—the only thing which could be controlled by women, considering babies grow within their own bodies—was kept firmly within the sphere of male control instead.

The concept of a "love marriage" is relatively recent, and is still considered taboo in many parts of the world, where the possibility of marriage reaching beyond economic stability for women, and the respectability and heirs it affords men, is tantamount to betrayal of one's own family.

So, despite Hollywood's best efforts to make marriage appear the epitome of romance, I can't quite get past matrimony's essentialism: that it stems from the kind of institutionalised inequality between genders that saw women as the property of their husbands—and before that, the property of their fathers.

Yet, governments, businesses and popular culture continue to propagate the concept of a traditional marriage by legislating against anything that could possibly disrupt this apparent "ideal," and also actively discriminating against those who, for whatever reason, are not married, or are not allowed to (hello, gay couples).

Former Families Minister Kevin Andrews went as far as to hand out $200 relationship counselling vouchers, hoping that many de facto couples would no doubt make society proud and get married.

He has also urged de facto couples to marry, which just shows how instrumental and determined the government is to force ideas of respectability onto the general public.

In reality, when it comes to marriage, men win and women lose, and women are starting to realise it.

For example, consider the falling rate of marriage. According to the Australian Bureau of Statistics, there were 4,282 fewer marriages in 2013 than the year before, a drop of 3.5 per cent.

The average marriage lasted 12.1 years in 2013, a slight decrease from 2012.

Women are also far more likely to initiate divorce than men, when given the choice. In Australia, the US and England, research has shown that women are behind roughly 70 per cent of all divorce proceedings. The reasons vary, however, it is interesting that with the introduction of no-fault divorce in 1975, it is women who began leaving.

Young, professional women are also choosing to live alone for longer, with recent Australian Institute of Family Studies data showing that women younger than 40 are choosing to live by themselves more often than men. In addition, those women who do live alone are 70 per cent more likely to have a tertiary degree, and 60 per cent more likely to work professionally than men in the same position.

It is no wonder that younger women, and especially those who have demanding and exciting jobs, have much to lose when they marry.

According to the most recent data released by the Australian Bureau of Statistics, the gender pay gap in Australia has reached a record high of 18.8 per cent. In real terms, this means that female employees are penalised almost $300 per week.

Now throw into the equation marriage and, what usually follows, children. Statistics show that even the most egalitarian households will ultimately conform to traditional gender roles, with women not only being forced out of the full time workforce—only 3 per cent of Australian families have a mother who works full time, as opposed to 60 per cent where the father is the primary breadwinner—but also taking on the brunt of domestic labour and childcare responsibilities.

To conclude: marriage is an institution based on the alliance between two unequal partners, which requires one partner, the husband, to be dominant and the wife to be subservient in order to function. The premise of the so-called perfect traditional marriage is rooted in the man having all economic control in the relationship, and thus, most of the control in general, as financial control leads to control of how the money is spent and how life is lived.

I know that many couples, including those who identify as feminist, continue to marry. Many of these couples will no doubt redefine the concept of marriage to suit their own needs and personalities, and can separate themselves from the historical makeup of this institution enough for it to make their relationship stronger.

In the end, what bothers me the most is not that marriage exists; I can see how for many people, the idea of being bound to someone legally, and perhaps spiritually, is a beautiful thing, and a public validation of each other's affections.

But until the entire structure of society changes (read: no more patriarchy), the institution of marriage will remain a reflection of that structure, which, unfortunately, continues to penalise women for their gender. And for me, that's just something I cannot separate from what marriage is supposed to represent: complete and utter equality between two people who love each other.

> *"Throughout this country's history, Americans have repeatedly contested what marriage is all about and what form it should take."*

There Is No Such Thing as "Traditional" Marriage

Janet I. Tu

In the following viewpoint, Janet I. Tu focuses on the many forms and reasons for marriage throughout history. The author puts the modern-day concept of "traditional" marriage in its rightful context. She notes that marriage has had many purposes and intentions from its beginning, and that a notable change today is the decline in number of marriages. Janet I. Tu is a writer and the assistant features editor for arts and entertainment at the Seattle Times, *based in Seattle, Washington.*

As you read, consider the following questions:

1. What does the author say Christian marriage was actually based on?
2. According to the author, how has politics also formed the idea of marriage?
3. How did the rise of the Roman Catholic Church affect the institution of marriage, according to the viewpoint?

"'Traditional' Marriage? History Shows People Wed in Many Ways for Many Reasons," by Janet I. Tu, *Seattle Times*, March 29, 2004. Reprinted by permission.

In ancient Greece and Rome, marriage was primarily a way for the upper class to pass down family property.

In early American Colonial times, a man and woman were considered married if they simply said they were.

And it wasn't until about a century ago that the practice of marrying for romantic love became widespread.

In the national debate over gay marriage, supporters say marriage is about love and commitment between two people, and that to deny gay men and lesbians the public sanction and legal benefits of marriage violates their civil rights.

Many opponents argue that legalizing gay marriage amounts to disavowing a cornerstone of Western society—an institution they say has historically been between one man and one woman, and designed primarily for child-rearing.

A look at the history of marriage in Western civilization, especially since the rise of Christianity, shows that it has, indeed, largely been between a man and a woman and designed, in large part, for the production of children. At the same time, it's an institution that has constantly evolved in response to changing social and political forces.

"Marriage is not an institution that's etched in stone," said Steven Mintz, a University of Houston professor who specializes in family history. "Whenever people talk about traditional marriage or traditional families, historians throw up their hands, because we say: 'When and where?'"

Marriage has existed since the earliest civilizations, with records of ancient Mesopotamia showing evidence of ceremonies and contracts. The institution likely has endured over the centuries because it fulfilled so many social and personal functions: It offered a structure that determined how property was to be handed down, how labor was to be divided, how children were to be cared for, how companionship would be assured.

Different cultures in different times have practiced many forms of marriage. The ancient Hebrews, for instance, practiced polygamy—a form of marriage once widespread among cultures worldwide. Until the 19th century, some Native American cultures allowed two men to essentially marry, provided one underwent a ritual that resulted in his being considered a crossed-gender or mixed-gender person.

"If you're talking about the history of the world and not just the last two centuries, the proportion of the world populated by monogamous households were a tiny, tiny portion—just Western Europe and little settlements in North America," said Nancy Cott, professor of history at Harvard University.

"What we talk about as marriage—monogamy between a man and a woman that's supposed to be lifelong, unless something goes wrong, and where there's sexual faithfulness—that's a Christian idea."

Indeed, Christianity has provided the foundation of what Western culture understands marriage to be today. It is largely this Christian tradition—the idea of marriage between one man and one woman as being what God intended—that is at odds with the idea of gay marriage.

Yet even within this Christian context, historians say, the purposes and functions of marriage have constantly evolved.

In America, for example, founded on Judeo-Christian values, people have debated everything from whether people of different races could marry, to the role of men and women in marriage.

Throughout this country's history, says Mintz, "Americans have repeatedly contested what marriage is all about and what form it should take."

A Matter of Class, Contract

In ancient Greece and Rome, the foundations of Western civilization, marriage was regarded as a civil contract, conducted mainly by the propertied class to perpetuate the family line and produce legitimate heirs.

The state did not get involved—marriages were considered a private contract arranged between a bridegroom and the father of a bride, and could be terminated at any time by either partner.

Though marriage was a heterosexual union, and a person could have only one spouse, that didn't preclude married men from having concubines who might bear their illegitimate children. It was also acceptable for men—married or not—to have sexual relationships with other males.

In the ancient Greek city of Thebes, for instance, one of its most celebrated military forces was the Sacred Theban Band, which was said to have been formed of 150 pairs of male lovers, some of whom probably had wives, said Lawrence Bliquez, a classics professor at the University of Washington.

Though homosexuality was practiced, ancient Greeks and Romans didn't think of it as either innate or exclusive of relationships with people of the opposite gender. Thus, exclusive same-sex relationships—in which men would not marry, produce offspring and perpetuate the family line—were probably unacceptable, said Bliquez.

Rise of the Church

It wasn't until the Roman Empire collapsed, around the 5th century, that the Catholic Church—for centuries the only Christian church—further extended its influence. The church elevated marriage from a civil contract to a sacred union, forming the basis of marriage laws in most Western countries.

In the 5th century, the church began clearly articulating the values and practices the faithful were expected to apply to their daily lives, including marriage. Referring to biblical passages, church leaders spoke of marriage as an unbreakable covenant between a man and a woman made "one flesh" by God.

They saw a passage from the Book of Ephesians, equating the love of a husband for his wife to that of Christ's love for his church, as a basis for the sacredness of marriage.

Still, marriages in the early Middle Ages, between the years 400 and 800, were "pretty ad hoc," said Theresa Earenfight, assistant professor of history at Seattle University. Fledgling states "couldn't run themselves then, much less manage marriage."

The church, too, had not yet developed a strong central infrastructure, so marriages were largely celebrated according to existing local customs. The church considered couples married if they simply gave their consent to each other and consummated the relationship.

From about 800 to 1200, as both church and states grew in power, the Catholic Church began enforcing more of its rules on marriage—prohibiting marriage between close relatives, for example, and stipulating that marriage could only be between a willing man and woman.

Church law and royal law worked together to form increasingly detailed laws surrounding marriage—such as rules for inheritance and dowries. Divorces became harder to obtain. In 1215, marriage was officially declared one of the church's seven sacraments, holy rites that include baptism and penance. After about 1200, the distinctions between church and state weddings began to blur, with most Christians getting married in church, and most states recognizing church marriages. In the mid-1500s, churches required marriages to be performed in public, by a church representative and before two witnesses.

But even as a sacrament, marriage still had its earthly purposes.

For the ruling class in Europe, for example, it remained a way to forge political alliances. In 1540, for instance, King Henry VIII of England, believing he needed an ally to repel threats from France, married Anne of Cleves, whose brother led the Protestants in western Germany. Six months later, after a French threat failed to materialize, the king had the marriage annulled.

For both the upper and aspiring classes, marriage was a way to gain capital—mainly through dowries. And for lower-class families, marriage could increase property holdings by merging one family's land with a neighbor's.

Beginning around the 16th century, the primary purpose of marriage shifted, to that of building the family as a labor force. At the same time, the Protestant Reformation brought about the idea that marriage should focus more on child-rearing.

Critics of the Catholic Church said its emphasis on chastity and a celibate clergy didn't place enough importance on marriage and the raising of children, said Mintz, the University of Houston historian.

The Reformation raised the idea of families as "little churches" that would educate children—an ideal that wouldn't flourish in practice until two centuries later.

Love and Marriage

Around the 18th century, the Enlightenment movement took hold, shaped by intellectuals who placed greater value on human logic and reason than on faith and church doctrine.

As freedom and personal fulfillment became more important, people began thinking marriage should be for love—not arranged, but rather, entered into freely.

That isn't to say earlier marriages didn't provide comfort and companionship—many people did, indeed, come to love their spouses.

"But people thought it was crazy to marry for such a fragile reason as love," said Stephanie Coontz, a historian with the Evergreen State College and co-chairwoman of the Council on Contemporary Families, a nonpartisan group of family researchers.

"If love could grow out of it, that was wonderful. But that was gravy."

It wasn't until about a century ago that that notion of marrying for romantic love became widespread practice.

Married in America

In the United States, as in Europe, how and why people married, who was allowed to marry, and how marriages functioned has also continually evolved.

In early American Colonial days, when there were few courts or churches, marriages were informal by necessity—many got married by living together and declaring themselves husband and wife. Such common-law marriages are still allowed in 11 states and the District of Columbia, said Mintz, of the University of Houston.

Before the Civil War, slaves were considered property and thus could not marry legally, though many slaves held their own ceremonies.

After the war, many states banned interracial marriages. Also, in the early 1900s, when anti-Asian sentiment was high, a national law said women who married Asians—even US-born Asians—lost their citizenship. The US Supreme Court declared such laws unconstitutional in 1967.

The role of men and women in marriage also has evolved—from husband as legal head of household, to the now widespread notion that marriage should be between equals.

In Colonial times, marriage was "more a work unit than anything else," said David Popenoe, professor of sociology at Rutgers University and co-director of its National Marriage Project, a nonpartisan institute aimed at strengthening marriage through research. "As in any work unit, the idea was you needed a boss to make it work efficiently. So the men were the boss."

Coontz, the Evergreen State College professor, places the current debate over gay marriage in the context of Americans having "already turned our backs on thousands of years of history when we said women should be equal to men, marriage should be for love, and kids should have the right to choose who they want to marry."

She sees the debate as "really a question of which part of the history do we want to keep and which do we want to discard. We've already discarded a lot of it."

Popenoe agrees marriage has evolved but believes its most important function should be to provide a stable environment for raising children.

Research has shown, he said, that growing up with both a mother and a father is beneficial to children and thus to society.

Fewer Marriages Ahead?

Some scholars believe another evolution in marriage may be taking place in Western countries.

After the purpose of marriage became primarily love and happiness, people who fell out of love could—and increasingly did—get divorced. When marriage is driven by love, and divorce is an option, the breakup rate is high.

But "the most notable change in marriage in recent years is not divorce, but the decline in the number of marriages," Mintz said.

Indeed, the marriage rate in the US is half what it was when it peaked right after World War II.

To some extent, Mintz sees marriage in Western cultures returning to a kind of "pre-modern pattern" where upper-class people marry to protect their holdings while many others don't marry at all.

"There's kind of an irony that we as a society are fixating on marriage," he said, "when in fact much of what is going on is happening outside of marriage."

Periodical and Internet Sources Bibliography

The following articles have been selected to supplement the diverse views presented in this chapter.

Ryan Anderson, "Marriage: What Is It, Why It Matters, and the Consequences of Redefining It," Heritage.org, March 11, 2013. https://www.heritage.org/marriage-and-family/report/marriage -what-it-why-it-matters-and-the-consequences-redefining-it

Amanda Barroso, "More Than Half of Americans Say Marriage Is Important but Not Essential to Leading a Fulfilling Life," Pew Research Center, February 14, 2020. https://www.pewresearch.org /fact-tank/2020/02/14/more-than-half-of-americans-say-marriage -is-important-but-not-essential-to-leading-a-fulfilling-life

Lita Epstein, "Marriage vs. Common Law Marriage: What's the Difference?" Investopedia.com, July 28, 2020. https://www .investopedia.com/financial-edge/0210/marriage-vs.-common -law-what-it-means-financially.aspx

Maggie Gallagher, "What Is Marriage For? The Public Purposes of Marriage Now," *Louisiana Law Review*, Spring 2002. https:// digitalcommons.law.lsu.edu/cgi/viewcontent .cgi?article=5933&context=lalrev&httpsredir=1&referer=

A. W. Geiger and Gretchen Livingston, "8 Facts About Love and Marriage in America," Pew Research Center, February 13, 2019. https://www.pewresearch.org/fact-tank/2019/02/13/8-facts -about-love-and-marriage/

Scott Hirschfield, "What Is Marriage For?" Beacon Press. https:// www.beacon.org/Assets/PDFs/WhatIsMarriageForPt1dg.pdf

Ivy Jacobsen, "13 Legal Benefits of Marriage," *The Knot*, July 13, 2020. https://www.theknot.com/content/benefits-of-marriage

Lonelyplanet.com, "31 Unusual Love and Marriage Customs from Around the World," February 26, 2020

Lumen Learning.com, "Functions of Marriage." https://courses .lumenlearning.com/culturalanthropology/chapter/functions-of -marriage

Nancy Mattia and Andrea Park, "45 Fascinating Wedding Traditions from Around the World," *Brides*, November 6, 2020. https://www.brides.com/gallery/wedding-traditions-around-the-world

Kim Parker, "Among LGBT American, Bisexuals Stand Out When It Comes to Identity, Acceptance," Pew Research Center, February 20, 2015. https://www.pewresearch.org/fact-tank/2015/02/20/among-lgbt-americans-bisexuals-stand-out-when-it-comes-to-identity-acceptance/

Psychology Today, "Marriage." https://www.psychologytoday.com/us/basics/marriage

The Week, "The Origins of Marriage," January 1, 2007. https://theweek.com/articles/528746/origins-marriage

W. Bradford Wilcox, Nicholas H. Wolfinger, and Charles E. Stokes, "The Role of Culture in Declining Marriage Rates," Institute for Family Studies, March 10, 2016. https://ifstudies.org/blog/the-role-of-culture-in-declining-marriage-rates

OPPOSING
VIEWPOINTS®
SERIES

CHAPTER 2

Who Gets Married and Why?

Chapter Preface

In Western societies, the Judeo-Christian religious system has organized marriage and family structure around the Bible's creation myth of the first man and woman, Adam and Eve, and their lifetime commitment to each other. The nuclear family, with a man, a woman, and their offspring, is the primary unit upon which everything is built, according to this belief system.

Currently, however, sociologists dispute how much this idealized notion of family reflects reality. Sociologist Stephanie Coontz argues that American families, for instance, have perhaps always been defined by economic rather than idealized circumstances. Additionally, she theorizes that since the twentieth century, marriage has become an increasingly unstable institution, as people have started to base partner selection largely on ideals of love, compatibility, and affection.

There are many theories about how marriage partners actually choose each other. One suggests that men and women compete in a "marriage market" influenced by factors including educational level. Studies show that partners prefer marriage partners with a similar educational level to their own. One interesting finding is that those couples with the lowest educational level tend to divorce the most. Studies show that demographics such as social class also affect the selection of marriage partners.

The viewpoint selections in this chapter concentrate on the social and demographic aspects that surround the institution of marriage and also their impact on societies.

> *"When asked about what kinds of things are important for a successful marriage, 44% of adults say shared religious beliefs are 'very important.'"*

Religion Plays an Important Role in Marriage
Pew Research Center

In the following viewpoint, the Pew Research Center reports on the importance of religious affiliation in modern marriages and families. The author examines levels of religious engagement between partners and within families. Observations on participation, desired shared belief systems, and engagement in religious practices are discussed. The Pew Research Center is an American think tank located in Washington, DC, that provides nonpartisan information on social issues, demographics, and public opinion.

As you read, consider the following questions:

1. How important is religion in most modern marriages, according to the viewpoint?
2. How does religion affect family relations?
3. According to the author, are interfaith modern marriages usually successful?

"Religion in Marriages and Families," Pew Research Center, Washington, DC. October 26, 2016. https://www.pewforum.org/2016/10/26/religion-in-marriages-and-families/. Used in accordance with Pew Research Center reuse policy. http://www.pewresearch.org/terms-and-conditions/. Usage in no way implies endorsement.

Adults in religiously mixed marriages are, by and large, less religious than their counterparts who are married to spouses who share their faith. They attend religious services less often, pray less frequently, tend to be less likely to believe in God with absolute certainty and are less inclined to say religion is very important in their lives.

People in religiously mixed marriages also discuss religious matters with their spouses less frequently than those who are in religiously matched marriages. Religion does not, however, appear to be the source of much strife in mixed relationships; while those in mixed marriages report somewhat higher levels of disagreement about religion, majorities nonetheless say religious disagreements are not common in their marriages.

When asked about what kinds of things are important for a successful marriage, 44% of adults say shared religious beliefs are "very important." By this metric, shared religion is seen as more important for a good marriage than shared political attitudes, but substantially less important than shared interests, good sex and a fair division of household labor. There are, however, significant subsets of the population who place a higher priority on religion within marriage; most people who are highly religious themselves say shared religious faith is critical to a good marriage, and women are much more likely than men to say the religion of a prospective spouse is likely to factor prominently in a decision about whether to get married.

The data also show that when parents attend religious services, they mostly do so with their children—especially if they are in a religiously matched marriage. Religiously affiliated parents married to spouses who share their faith also are more likely than intermarried parents to pray or read scripture with their children.

The remainder of this chapter explores attitudes about and experiences with religion in family life.

Religiously Intermarried People Are Generally Less Religious Than Those Married to Spouse with Same Religion

Religiously affiliated people in mixed marriages tend to be less religious than those who are married to spouses who share their religious identity. Among Catholics married to other Catholics, for instance, seven-in-ten are highly religious, according to an index of key measures used to determine levels of religious observance in the Religious Landscape Study (including frequency of worship attendance, frequency of prayer, belief in God and self-described importance of religion in one's own life). By comparison, only about half of Catholics married to non-Catholics are highly religious.

Of course, it is impossible to know for sure the direction of the causal arrow in the relationship between religious observance and religious intermarriage. Marrying someone from a different faith might serve to make people less religious. Alternatively, it could be that people who are not particularly religious to begin with are more likely to marry a spouse with a different religion. Or it could be some combination of both factors.

In any case, while intermarriage is linked with lower rates of religious observance among those who are affiliated with a religion, there is little evidence that the relationship goes in the opposite direction for those who are religiously unaffiliated. That is, being married to a religiously affiliated spouse seems to have little impact on the religiosity of religious "nones." [*Nones* is a term used to refer to those who do not claim a religious affiliation.] Just 13% of religious "nones" married to a religiously affiliated spouse are highly religious, which is only modestly higher than the 9% of "nones" married to fellow "nones" who are highly religious.

THE LAS VEGAS WEDDING

Dun dunnnnn...

You and your special someone are tying the knot, yay! Whether it's eloping on a secret rendezvous or planning an elaborate ceremony for hundreds of your family and friends, there is no place quite like Las Vegas to make it official.

Before you say "I do," we vow to show you why you should have your wedding in Vegas.

Get married literally anywhere, anytime and any way you want.

Whether you're wanting your first kiss as a married couple to be in front of the Bellagio fountains, in Red Rock Canyon or 550 feet in the air on the High Roller, Vegas is the place you can get an experience totally custom to what you and your fiancée want on that special day.

Your planning experience will be easy and convenient.

Maybe you missed the booking window for your city, or you're having trouble planning it all yourself. No worries, the ease and convenience for you and your guests are some of the most practical selling points as to why you should have your wedding in Vegas. Not only are there limitless hotel options to accommodate your guests and their individual budgets, but we also have a huge selection of direct flights arriving and departing McCarran International Airport every day. Plus, most of the wedding packages at hotels on the Strip arm you with a personal wedding planner to help make your dream day a reality

Bachelorette party? Reception? Honeymoon? We're a one-stop wedding shop.

Convenience, efficiency, a straight up obsession with this city— whatever the reason, Vegas is the perfect spot for all your wedding festivities. Those trying to plan their bachelor or bachelorette parties, reception, honeymoon and more will be happy at the ease of setting up these events in Vegas. Plus, guests only have to pay for travel once to experience the whole shebang. Not to mention bachelor and bachelorette parties in Vegas aren't famous for nothing.

The best weddings are (and always have been) Vegas weddings. We're here to make your day not only incredibly special, but exactly how you've always imagined it going down.

"10 Reasons to Have Your Wedding in Vegas," visitlasvegas.com.

For a Successful Marriage, Shared Religious Beliefs Prized About as Much as Adequate Income, Less Than Sex and Shared Interests

Overall, 44% of US adults say shared religious beliefs are "very important" for a successful marriage. By that metric, religion is seen as about as important for a successful marriage as is having an adequate income or having children, and it is considered less important than having shared interests, a satisfying sexual relationship or an equitable distribution of housework.

Among married people, the survey finds big differences in the perceived importance of religion depending on the nature of one's marriage. Nearly two-thirds of religiously affiliated respondents with spouses who share their faith (64%) say shared religious beliefs are key to a successful marriage. Far fewer married people in interfaith relationships see shared religious beliefs as central to a successful marriage.

The data also show that among those who are highly religious—including both married and unmarried respondents—shared religious beliefs are prized in marriage almost as much as shared interests and about as much as a satisfying sex life and sharing household chores. Far smaller shares of those who are not highly religious see shared religious beliefs as essential for a good marriage. Having children also is seen as critical for a good marriage by more of those who are highly religious than those who are not.

While nearly half of married people say shared religious faith is crucial for a successful marriage, just 27% of married adults say their spouse's religion was, in fact, a "very important" factor in deciding whether to marry them specifically. Roughly a third of religiously affiliated adults who are married to someone of the same faith (36%) say their spouse's religion factored prominently in their decision to marry, while far fewer intermarried adults—and just one-in-twenty religious "nones" married to fellow "nones"—say the same.

Among those who are not currently married, the survey finds the religion of a potential spouse is more important to women than it is to men. Nearly four-in-ten women say their potential spouse's religion would be a "very important" factor if they were considering marriage, while just 26% of single men say the same.

Not surprisingly, the data also show that the religion of a potential spouse would be far more important to highly religious people than to single people who are not highly religious. Still, even among the highly religious, roughly a quarter say the religion of their prospective spouse would be only "somewhat important" to their decision, and one-in-five say it would be "not too" or "not at all" important.

Among Both Men and Women, More Say Women Are the More Religious Half in Marriage

Roughly six-in-ten married people say they and their spouses are about equally religious. This includes about three-quarters of "nones" married to spouses who are also religiously unaffiliated and nearly two-thirds of religiously affiliated adults married to a spouse from the same religion. Only about half of religiously affiliated adults married to someone from a different religion (46%) say they and their spouse are equally religious, and just 36% of those in a marriage combining one religiously affiliated spouse and one religious "none" say both spouses are equally religious.

Among those in this latter type of relationship, it is typically the religiously affiliated spouse who is described as more religiously observant than the unaffiliated spouse. The data also show that in marriages in which one spouse is more religious than the other, wives generally are seen as more religious than husbands. About one-third of married women say they are more religious than their husbands, while a similar share of husbands say their wives are more religious than them. By contrast, just 8% of women and 10% of men say the husband is more religious in their marriage.

Most religiously affiliated people with spouses who share their religion say they attend religious services with their spouse. Attending services at a house of worship together is far less common among people married to a spouse from a different religion.

And among married "nones" whose spouses are also religiously unaffiliated, most say they rarely or never attend religious services at all.

Religious Disagreement Relatively Uncommon, Even in Intermarriages

Within marriages, religious discussion is most common among religiously affiliated adults who have spouses affiliated with the same religion. Nearly eight-in-ten (78%) in this group say they talk about religion "a lot" or "some" with their spouse; religious discussions are less common among those married to a spouse with a different religion (or no religion) and among religious "nones" married to fellow "nones."

Religious disagreement is most common in religiously mixed marriages; for example, one-third of those in marriages pairing a religious "none" with a religiously affiliated spouse have at least some disagreements about religion. Still, in all kinds of marital combinations, religious discord is the exception rather than the rule; majorities in all types of pairings say they disagree with their spouse about religion "not much" or "not at all."

Intermarried Parents Participate in Fewer Religious Activities with Their Children

Most parents attend worship services at least a few times a year, and their children typically attend with them. About two-thirds of all parents of children currently under 18 (65%) usually attend worship services with their kids, including roughly eight-in-ten evangelical (83%) and Catholic (78%) parents and two-thirds of mainline Protestant parents (67%). Religiously unaffiliated parents are less likely to attend religious services at all; roughly seven-in-ten (69%) say they seldom or never attend church (or did not answer the question about attendance).

Among married parents, those who share their spouse's religious affiliation are among the most likely to attend worship services with their children (83%). Intermarried parents and "nones" married to other "nones" are less likely to attend religious services, but when they do, they also mostly say they take their kids with them.

Religiously affiliated parents married to spouses who share their faith are most likely to pray or read scripture with their children and to send them to religious education programs. They also are more likely than others to say they do volunteer work with their children, though the gaps between religiously affiliated parents married to a spouse of the same faith and other kinds of couples are relatively modest on this question.

> "Marriage was based on the principle
> of division of labour, and gains from
> marriage were determined by how
> efficient this division was."

People Marry Because It Makes Economic Sense

Sumit Mishra

In the following viewpoint, Sumit Mishra argues that married people benefit economically, but many are forced to make sub-optimal choices. The author offers an overview of economic theories behind partner selection and the division of labor in marriages, both from a historic and a modern-day perspective. Mishra also includes a critique of these theories, noting that they are often oversimplified. Sumit Mishra is a scholar who writes on economic issues.

As you read, consider the following questions:

1. What, according to the viewpoint, is the driving force behind marriages?
2. What is meant by a "marriage market"?
3. Who are some of the economists who have devised theories on marriage, according to the author?

"The Economics of Marriage," by Sumit Mishra, Live Mint, HT Media Limited, August 20, 2016. Reprinted by permission.

Finding a suitable partner can be a really painful business. Economists have devised methods to understand this process. The story goes back to the father of economics, Adam Smith. He wrote about division of labour for a pin factory, arguing that it is better to have specialized pin-makers instead of having equal number of general handymen.

Economics commentator Tim Harford extends this argument in his book *The Logic of Life* to marriage and makes an emphatic claim that "the family has rational roots. It is the oldest pin factory of all." People marry because it makes economic sense.

The idea that rational calculations may underpin romantic relationships goes back to the 1970s when Nobel Prize-winning economist Gary Becker first postulated an economic model of marriage, arguing that marriage was based on the principle of division of labour, and that gains from marriage were determined by how efficient this division was.

In Becker's model, finding a spouse is based on two core principles. First, he assumes that the exchange between the couple is voluntary. Second, that there are people—on Internet boards, classified ads of newspapers—looking for other people, signifying the presence of a market. There is a demand for prospective spouses and an abundant supply of hopefuls.

In Becker's own words, "According to the economic approach, a person decides to marry when the utility expected from marriage exceeds that expected from remaining single or from additional search for a more suitable mate. Similarly, a married person terminates his (or her) marriage when the utility anticipated from becoming single or marrying someone else exceeds the loss in utility from separation, including losses due to physical separation from one's children, division of joint assets, legal fees, and so forth. Since many persons are looking for mates a market in marriages is said to exist."

Marriage, sadly, is not the final outcome between two people who decide to be together. Who will go out to work? Who will do the household chores? Will they have kids (and how many)? These questions need to be answered once two people decide to marry.

The answer to the first two questions lies in division of labour, according to the Beckerian model. The one with comparative advantage at earning wages will go out and work; the other person has to do the dishes and probably stay at home.

The simplicity of the Beckerian model has appealed to many economists who have subsequently ventured into this arena with their toolbox. Some of them, though, are beginning to find that Becker may have oversimplified a bit too much.

Implicit in the Beckerian marriage market model is the fact that everything that happens post-marriage is determined while choosing the partner. This is obviously one of the weak links of this model. The truth is that whoever, within the marriage, has the greater share of resources or makes more money often calls the shots on most decisions.

In this case, the other person, if (s)he is able to foresee that their pay-offs from getting married are lower, can refuse the marriage and not getting married may be an equilibrium outcome.

Robert Pollak of Washington University, St. Louis, in a new National Bureau of Economic Research working paper, shows that equilibrium within a marriage market is determined by how someone can foresee the gains (or tribulations) from the prospective marriage. Foresight may ruin the marriage.

Another key assumption in the Becker marriage model is that families pool their resources, optimizing a single objective function for the couple, in which only these pooled resources affect the choices made by the family.

In a 1997 study, Pollak, Shelly Lundberg and Terence Wales put this pooling hypothesis to an empirical test in which they examined the impact of a child benefit programme in the UK in the 1970s.

Until Margaret Thatcher assumed office, the programme paid money to all families with kids via tax benefits, typically to the husband. The Thatcher government restructured this programme and decided to pay the mothers cash. If pooling did

Miscegenation Laws

To understand [miscegenation] laws, it is critical to understand the ways in which people of color in the US have been dehumanized, tortured, and exploited for centuries. Like Jim Crow laws, which were established in the late 19th century, miscegenation laws aimed to uphold the false sanctity of whiteness while simultaneously disenfranchising an entire group of people. Although slavery had been abolished, the belief that black people are inherently inferior to whites was still deeply embedded into American society. The pervasive narrative that black people are inherently violent and animalistic led to the formation of hate groups that would become violent vehicles for white Southern resistance—with the most infamous being the Ku Klux Klan. Formed in 1865, members of the KKK were responsible for the bombings, beatings, and lynching of black people and activists who were working toward laws that promoted racial equity. Even after black people were theoretically promised separate but equal public facilities as a result of 1896's landmark Supreme Court ruling *Plessy v. Ferguson*, discrimination and violence designed to advance white supremacy continued.

It wasn't until 1967 that the Supreme Court ruled that state miscegenation laws were unconstitutional in the landmark case *Loving v. Virginia*. "The freedom to marry, or not marry, a person of another race resides with the individual," wrote Chief Justice Earl Warren, "and cannot be infringed by the State." However, decades passed before every state in the US adopted the law of the land: only in 2000, the last hold out, Alabama, eliminated the (non-enforceable) rule.

By concocting and enforcing laws that forbid interracial relationships, racial persecution became further exacerbated. These beliefs carried over into this generation, and the inherent discriminatory beliefs that drove miscegenation laws will continue to make interracial relationships a source of fodder for racists. Fifty years after this historic decision, interracial dating and marriage has steadily risen. However, it is sometimes still sensationalized and stigmatized. Although many claim to no longer harbor racial bias toward black people, a series of recent studies of predominantly white college students found that participants showed disgust for interracial couples.

"Miscegenation Laws in the United States, Explained," *Teen Vogue*, Conde Nast, November 29, 2017.

work, everything else remaining the same, there shouldn't be any shift in household expenditure pattern.

Pollak and others compared the expenditure patterns before and after the restructuring, and found a significant increase in expenditure on children and women's clothing when women were paid.

Becker also ignored the fact that the utilities of spouses are not the same, and that bargaining within marriage determines the equilibrium outcome. In a 2009 *Journal of Development Economics* paper, Siwan Anderson and Mukesh Eswaran show that market wages have far greater bargaining power than that of household work.

Using data from rural Bangladesh, Anderson and Eswaran argue that working on one's own farm is not so much better than staying at home, and that true autonomy comes only from having an independent source of income.

Bargaining within marriage is crucially hinged upon the ability of the person to find an easy exit from the marriage.

During the 1970s, divorce rates in the US started increasing. A combination of factors—including divorce legislation, the availability of contraceptive pills and the opening up of the labour market to women—delayed the age at marriage and lowered the barriers to exit the marriage.

The rising female labour force participation within the country contributed to the rise in divorces. If women had no opportunities outside the marriage, they would have resigned themselves to the drudgery of staying within a cruel marriage.

Race and caste barriers further complicate the marriage market. In a 2010 paper, Daniel Ariely of Duke University and his co-authors, using data from more than 20,000 people who used a dating website, showed that race played a significant role in the choices people made. Economists Abhijit Banerjee, Esther Duflo and others examined data on people who placed ads in Bengali newspapers and found a strong in-caste preference.

Data from the 2011 Indian Human Development Survey shows that 95% of women married within their own caste and 41% reported to have no say in their marriage.

Becker's marriage model, for all its attractiveness and simplicity, is inadequate in explaining why so many people are forced to make sub-optimal choices when they get married. Even if rational calculations play a role, they are not the sole driver of the marriage market. Social norms and institutions, biases and power relations influence the market heavily.

> *"When it comes to the processes behind perhaps our most significant life choice—choosing a romantic partner—science knows surprisingly little."*

Scientists Understand Very Little About How We Choose Marriage Partners

Brendan Zietsch

In the following viewpoint, Brendan Zietsch argues that the scientific research conducted to understand marriage partner selection has been extraordinarily scant. The author examines the various scientific theories regarding heterosexual marriage alliances that do exist and concludes that much is left to individual differences in people's preferences, despite basic theories. Brendan Zietsch is a research fellow studying evolutionary and genetic approaches to human behavior at the University of Queensland in Australia.

"How Do We Choose a Partner?" by Brendan Zietsch, The Conversation, May 26, 2016. https://theconversation.com/how-do-we-choose-a-partner-58217. Licensed under CC BY-ND 4.0 International.

As you read, consider the following questions:

1. What theories does the author delve into regarding partner selection?
2. What differences does the author talk about regarding the two sexes via partner selection?
3. What does the author have to say about individual differences in partner selection?

We know a lot about why people choose different brands of dishwashing detergent, because companies spend billions of dollars investigating who buys what. But when it comes to the processes behind perhaps our most significant life choice—choosing a romantic partner—science knows surprisingly little.

One reason partner choice is hard to understand is because it's a two-way street. A person can choose any dishwashing detergent they like, because the detergent has no choice in the matter, but choosing a partner doesn't work that way. We need to understand not only what kind of people person A prefers, but also what kind of people prefer person A, how those two groups overlap, the influence of other competitors trying to elbow in on person A's turf, and so on. It's all very complex.

So let's start simple(ish). Accordingly, I'll focus on Western heterosexuals, on whom most of the research has been done.

What Everyone Wants

There's nothing that everyone wants in a partner—everyone has their own idiosyncratic preferences—but there are characteristics most men or women find attractive.

As depressing as it is, a big part of romance and attraction is physical. It's not just that everyone's a unique snowflake destined to find their special complementary snowflake. Different people tend to agree a fair bit about who is more and less physically attractive, which sadly means there are haves and have-nots in the looks lottery.

Men's preferences, on the other hand, are dominated by a strong predilection for slimness (though not ultra-thinness). Much has been made of men's apparent attraction to low waist-to-hip ratios (hourglass figures), but more recent research suggests it is just a byproduct of slim women tending to have low waist-to-hip ratios.

Public dismay about society's heavy emphasis on beauty tends to focus on body image issues, but research suggests a person's face is even more important to overall attractiveness. This might sound nice, but isn't really when you consider it's harder to change a face than a body.

Both men and women tend to prefer geometrically average faces (that is, faces close to the shape of the average face for their gender, as opposed to distinctive faces).

People also tend to prefer left-right symmetrical faces, but this aspect of beauty is often oversold. Symmetry has only a tiny impact on facial attractiveness, accounting for only around 1% of the total variation. So don't worry too much about your wonky nostril or huge left eye or whatever.

Men also prefer feminine female faces. This typically means, for example, big eyes and a small chin—think Miranda Kerr.

Strangely, women don't tend to prefer masculine male faces: on average they show no strong preference either way. If anything, they prefer more feminine male faces, thus your Biebers and your Depps being international sex symbols.

It's not all about looks, of course. Both men and women say they'd prefer a kind and intelligent partner. And both sexes like a good sense of humour. But there's a catch: women want a man who is funny, while men prefer a woman who finds them funny.

Individual Preferences

There is plenty of individuality in preferences as well, some of which is based on the extent to which we value different traits in a partner. Few women prefer narrow shoulders on a man, but plenty don't place much importance on shoulder width. Instead they see nice eyes, brains or jokes as more important.

So what causes individuals to differ in the traits they value more and less?

My colleagues and I studied thousands of genetically identical and nonidentical twins who ranked 13 traits (such as physical attractiveness, kindness, intelligence) in terms of their importance in a partner.

We found that the genetically identical twin pairs had more similar rankings than genetically nonidentical twins. This implies that genes influence people's preference rankings.

We've shown a similar thing with specific physical preferences, too, such as whether you prefer beard or clean-shaven, tall or short, long hair or short hair, or whether you tend to prefer digitally masculinised or feminised facial photos. All these preferences are more similar in genetically identical twin pairs than in nonidentical twin pairs, again implying genetic influence on our individual preferences.

Actual Partner Choices

So how do these genetically influenced preferences translate into who actually partners with whom?

Since identical twins have similar partner preferences, we'd expect them to have similar partners as well, right? Well, they don't—at least not in any meaningful way that my colleagues and I could detect among thousands of twins and their partners.

This means there's a lot of mismatched partners.

If this mismatch between genetically influenced preferences and actual partners emerged only in humans, we might wonder if modern society has somehow divorced our partner choices from our inherited preferences. However, the same pattern of results has been observed in species of birds that, like humans, form pair bonds.

So what's the deal with the mismatch? Well, this is an open scientific question, but it probably boils down to the fact we can't all get what we want. For one thing, most of us don't meet enough people to find someone who fulfils all of our preferences. So right away we're dealing with the best of the available, rather than a perfect match.

But what are the chances that the best of the available will be interested in us anyway, with our wonky nostril and obvious character flaws?

And then there are those other guys or gals with preferences similar to ours, trying to get in on this action as well, telling better jokes at Friday drinks and generally leaving us for dead.

So we settle for someone who doesn't really match our preferences too well, but is basically alright, we suppose. Hopefully.

This must be part of the reason relationships are hard and often stressful. The consequences of mismatch between preferences and actual partners aren't well studied in humans, but in finches females paired with a non-preferred partner were found to have stress hormone levels three times higher than those paired with a preferred partner.

Judging by the amount of relationship dysfunction and breakdown in our society (estimated to cost A$14 billion per year in Australia), this phenomenon probably isn't limited to birds.

So it would be great to see more studies about the process of partner selection, what causes partners to match or not, and the consequences of mismatch. There's so much we don't understand, and the immense complexity of the process makes the search for answers both intimidating and exciting. Much like the search for a partner, I guess.

> *"There are certain conditions that have to be met for a couple to be considered married by common law."*

Common Law Marriage Is Different from Marriage

Lita Epstein

In the following viewpoint, Lita Epstein explains the differing common law marriage requirements in various states. What is true in Arizona may not be true for these kinds of unions in New York, it follows. Neither should common law marriages be confused with traditional marriages or with civil unions, which were primarily a way to confer rights on same-sex couples before the era of legal same-sex marriages. Lita Epstein is the author of more than 40 books, including several financial books in the "Dummies" series. She has won numerous awards for her writing.

As you read, consider the following questions:

1. What is the difference between common law marriage and civil unions, according to the viewpoint?
2. How does common law marriage differ by various states?
3. What does it take for common law marriage to be considered legal?

"Marriage vs. Common Law Marriage: What's the Difference?" by Lita Epstein, Dotdash Publishing Family, September 6, 2019. Reprinted by permission.

- Rhode Island—Both man and woman must intend to be married and act as if they are (i.e., live together and present themselves as married to friends and family).
- South Carolina—Allows for marriage without a valid license. No specific laws on common law marriage.
- Texas—Both members of the couple must consent to be married, live together, and tell others they are married.
- Utah—Both partners must be able to agree to the marriage, and others must know them as a married couple.

In addition, some states have "grandfathered" common law marriages, meaning that only those unions that meet the state requirements for a common law marriage by a specified date will be recognized. Those states and dates are:

- Alabama—January 1, 2017
- Georgia—January 1, 1997
- Idaho—January 1, 1996
- Ohio—October 10, 1991
- Oklahoma—November 1, 1998
- Pennsylvania—January 1, 2005 (in addition, partners must exchange vows to be married)

What Is the Financial Impact of a Common Law Marriage?

Couples recognized as married by common law enjoy many of the same benefits as legally married couples, provided they have lived in a state that recognizes common law for most of their marriage. These benefits include:

- Eligibility to receive Social Security benefits—but they will need to prove the number of years they lived together in a common law state
- Qualifying for employer benefits through their spouse (i.e., health insurance)
- Exemption from the gift tax

- Unlimited marital exemptions for their estate—up to the federal estate tax limit
- Claiming deductions for mortgage interest (if they co-own a house) and children (if applicable)
- Inheritance of their spouse's property as long as there is a valid will (but if a spouse dies without a will, their children and other family members will have inheritance rights and the surviving spouse will not have them)
- Use of a medical power of attorney designating their common law spouse as the person (rather than another family member) who will make medical decisions when they are incapable

Many of those benefits can help save money. Having one shared health plan instead of purchasing two separate plans, for example, could save thousands of dollars per year.

If a state recognizes common law marriage, and a couple does not want to be seen as married, they need to sign a living together contract—especially if they own property together or use the same last name.

While common law couples get to enjoy the financial and legal benefits of marriage in most cases, they may also be vulnerable to some of the potential downsides. If one spouse buys property on their own and the other spouse is not on the deed, for instance, the property can be sold without their consent. To circumvent this issue, major assets should be bought using co-ownership agreements. To be on the safe side, obligations and rights should be reviewed with an attorney who understands common law marriage.

The Bottom Line

Couples who move out of the state in which they established a common law marriage need to be aware that all states recognize a common law marriage that a couple legally entered into in another state. Still, after the move, they may want to sit down with an attorney in their new state to be sure they meet the legal obligations required to maintain their rights as a married couple. Keeping good records, especially if they move around a lot, can help when it comes to claiming federal benefits.

And if a common law couple decides to part ways, even though there is no "common law divorce," they will still need to have their relationship legally dissolved. This relates to the fact that a person in a common law marriage could be liable for providing the same type of support for their ex-spouse as someone in a legally binding marriage might be required to do after divorce.

> *"There are different reasons for pursuing a divorce versus an annulment. At the core, ending a marriage is generally because one or both spouses want to leave the union."*

There Are Important Distinctions Between Divorce and Annulment

Sheri Stritof

In the following viewpoint, Sheri Stritof argues that there are reasons for choosing annulment or divorce when ending a traditional Western marriage. Roughly speaking, a divorce recognizes that a marriage contract took place, whereas in an annulment, a marriage is made null and void and legally invalid. In addition, some religions define annulment and divorce differently from the legal definitions. The author lists the reasons for considering one or another when ending a marriage. Sheri Stritof is a writer and marriage counselor.

As you read, consider the following questions:

1. What are the largest differences between divorce and annulment, according to the viewpoint?
2. What are the connections annulment has to religion?
3. What legal aspects are there in annulment and divorce?

"The Difference Between a Divorce and an Annulment," by Sheri Stritof, Dotdash Publishing Family, February 5, 2020. Reprinted by permission.

There are two options for legally leaving a marriage: divorce and annulment, and there are several similarities and differences between the two.

Legally, some of the biggest differences include the type of evidence that is required to obtain an annulment vs. a divorce and the obligations to and from the former spouse with each ruling. Many religions define divorce and annulment as well, and the legal ruling does not necessarily have to align with the religious designation.

Divorce vs. Annulment

The biggest difference between a divorce and an annulment is that a divorce ends a legally valid marriage, while an annulment formally declares a marriage to have been legally invalid.

Divorce: A legal dissolving, termination, and ending of a legally valid marriage. A divorce ends a legal marriage and declares the spouses to be single again.

Annulment: A legal ruling that erases a marriage by declaring the marriage null and void and that the union was never legally valid. However, even if the marriage is erased, the marriage records remain on file. Note that a religious annulment is not a legal dissolution of a civil marriage.

Reasons

There are different reasons for pursuing a divorce versus an annulment. At the core, ending a marriage is generally because one or both spouses want to leave the union.

A divorce, which is much more common, is sought when the parties acknowledge that the marriage existed. An annulment is sought when one or both of the spouses believe that there was something legally invalid about the marriage in the first place.

Divorce

No-fault divorces, in which neither party is required to prove fault on the part of their spouse, is legal in every state, though some require that the couple live apart for a period of time before either can file. "Irreconcilable differences" is often cited as grounds for a no-fault divorce.

Common grounds cited for fault divorces can include things like adultery, imprisonment, or abandonment.

Regardless of type, the divorcing couple may still have disputes about property, finances, child custody, and more that must be settled through court orders. Fault divorces can lead to larger settlements for the party without fault.

Annulment

An annulment ends a marriage that at least one of the parties believes should never have taken place.

If the marriage took place despite unknown facts, such as a secret child, or even a secret illness, it may be voidable.

An annulment can also end a marriage if the marriage was not legal to begin with. This might occur if issues such as bigamy or incest made the marriage illegal.

The legal grounds for obtaining an annulment vary between states, but typically include reasons like the following:

- One or both spouses were forced or tricked into the marriage.
- One or both spouses were not able to make a decision to marry due to a mental disability, drugs, or alcohol.
- One or both spouses were already married at the time of the marriage (bigamy).
- One or both spouses were not of legal age to marry.
- The marriage was incestuous.
- Concealment of major issues such as drug abuse or a criminal history

Because one of these conditions must be met for an annulment to be granted, they are rare.

Length of the Marriage

Often, people assume that a very brief marriage can be ended with an annulment due to the short duration. However, legal experts disagree.

While many states will not grant an annulment after a certain length of time, there is not an automatic annulment granted to end a marriage because the couple wants to end it after a short period of time. The marriage still has to meet one or more of the conditions above in order for it to be annulled.

Legal Assistance

Both types of marriage dissolution can be fairly complicated from a legal standpoint, requiring costly and lengthy legal proceedings. And both start the same way, with one or both of the spouses formally asking the court for either a divorce or an annulment.

Either a divorce or an annulment can also be simple and low-cost if both parties agree to end the union without too many disputes or disagreements about how to do so.

After a Divorce or Annulment

Among the differences between the two types of marriage dissolution: After an annulment, the marriage is considered to have never legally happened. It is as if the clock is turned back to before the marriage.

After a divorce, the former spouses may still have obligations to each other, such as spousal support, joint childrearing, and division of shared property.

Finances

After a divorce, spouses are often entitled to a certain number of years of spousal support, alimony, or a portion of each others' profits or property gained during the marriage. With an annulment, in contrast, the parties are not really considered to have been valid spouses and are not entitled to these same rights. Instead, they will revert to the financial state they were in prior to the marriage.

Religious Rules

Many religions have guidelines regarding divorce and annulment. Often, permission is granted by religious clergy or by written guidelines. Obtaining permission to have an annulment or a divorce from your religious leaders is usually a completely separate process from the legal process.

The rules regarding divorce and annulment in your religion often determine whether one, both or neither of the partners has permission to marry again within the religion or in a religious ceremony or to participate in religious rituals.

A court of law may consider your religious marital status but does not have to recognize the religious determinations when making rulings about spousal support, property disputes, or any other legal issues.

Differences Between Annulments and Divorces

	Annulment	Divorce
State-required length of time before filing	Immediately allowed	May vary up to 1-2 years, depending on the state
Marriage existed	No	Yes
Children considered legitimate	Yes	Yes
Division of property	No	Yes
Alimony	No	Possible
Difficulty of legal qualification	High	Usually low
Grounds-specific	Yes	No (for no-fault divorces)
Marital status result	Single or unmarried	Divorced
Witness and proof required	Yes	No (for no-fault divorces)

Periodical and Internet Sources Bibliography

The following articles have been selected to supplement the diverse views presented in this chapter.

Census.gov, "Historical Marriage Trends from 1890-2010: A Focus on Race Differences." https://www.census.gov/content/dam /Census/library/working-papers/2012/demo/sehsd-wp2012-12_ presentation.pdf

Andrew Cherlin, "Demographic Trends in the United States: A Review of Research in the 2000's," ncbi.gov, June 2010. https:// pubmed.ncbi.nlm.nih.gov/22399825/

Encyclopedia.com, "Marriage." https://www.encyclopedia.com/social -sciences-and-law/anthropology-and-archaeology/customs-and -artifacts/marriage

Mary Kay Gilliland, "Family and Marriage," PB Pressbooks. https:// perspectives.pressbooks.com/chapter/family-and-marriage/

Dennis Hogan, "The Effects of Demographic Factors, Family Background, and Early Job Achievement on Age at Marriage, Springer.com. https://link.springer.com/article/10.2307/2060520

Rosemary Joyce, "Ask an Anthropologist About Marriage," *Psychology Today*, March 28, 2013. https://www .psychologytoday.com/us/blog/what-makes-us-human/201303 /ask-anthropologist-about-marriage

Living Anthropologically, "Is Marriage Natural?" 2017. https://www .livinganthropologically.com/anthropology-2017/is-marriage -natural/

Terry McFadden, "Same-Sex Marriage from an Anthropological View," Headstuff.org, September 23, 2015. https://www.headstuff .org/topical/same-sex-marriage-in-anthropology/

Pew Research Center, "The Decline of Marriage and Rise of New Families," November 18, 2010. https://www.pewsocialtrends .org/2010/11/18/the-decline-of-marriage-and-rise-of-new -families/

Richard V. Reeves and Christopher Pulliam, "Middle Class Marriage Is Declining and Likely Deepening Inequality," Brookings, March

11, 2020. https://www.brookings.edu/research/middle-class
-marriage-is-declining-and-likely-deepening-inequality/

Pamela J. Smock and Christine R. Schwartz, "The Demography
of Families: A Review of Patterns and Change," Wiley Online
Library, January 5, 2020. https://onlinelibrary.wiley.com/doi
/abs/10.1111/jomf.12612

tutor2u.net, "Families: Changing Patterns of Marriage." https://www
.tutor2u.net/sociology/reference/families-changing-patterns-of
-marriage

OPPOSING
VIEWPOINTS®
SERIES

CHAPTER 3

What Are the Issues Surrounding Marriage Today?

Chapter Preface

Today, the institution of marriage is facing many challenges and changes worldwide. Over the last few decades, the very nature of marriage has changed. As an example, many couples are choosing to live with their partners without the benefit of a legal marriage, and by and large, society is approving of this as a valid option. Also, couples who do legally marry currently have a 50 percent chance of remaining married, the equivalent of flipping a coin on one's wedding day.

Modern society also has removed the stigma once placed on divorce. Some researchers have blamed the ease with which couples can get divorced and the general disrespect for the institution of marriage for all of this, despite the fact that most people still express optimism in finding a life partner and in marrying them.

Beyond these changes, marriage as an institution faces other significant issues, such as the acknowledgment of same-sex marriage. Some powerful organizations still believe marriage should be designated as a union between a man and woman only.

The influence of patriarchal values on women's rights and freedoms within marriage is another issue, as is sexual violence and its role in marriage. Read on in this chapter for viewpoints focusing on the various problems and concerns facing our modern conceptions of matrimony.

> *"Perhaps what's most remarkable about this story is the amazing success of the wedding industry in propagating, despite obstacles, a new and ever-changing mass vision of what the 'traditional' American wedding should look like."*

Traditional Marriage Is Big Business in the United States

Janice M. Traflet

In the following viewpoint, Janice M. Traflet reviews a book about the commercialization of traditional weddings in the United States. The book's author, Vicki Howard, offers insights on why American heterosexual (and some same-sex) couples have made the marriage ceremony into lavish affairs that require expensive services as the new normal. Vicki Howard is a writer and a lecturer at the University of Essex in the United Kingdom. Janice M. Traflet is an assistant professor of marketing at Bucknell University.

"Book Review: *Brides Inc.: American Weddings and the Business of Tradition* by Vicki Howard, by Janice M. Traflet, EH.net, Economic History Association, February 2007. Reprinted by permission.

As you read, consider the following questions:

1. How much revenue is generated by the wedding industry, according to the viewpoint?
2. Why does the reviewer single out the organization of the book?
3. How do women transcend being victims of advertising and merchandising campaigns?

In *Brides Inc.*, Vicki Howard details in thought-provoking fashion the evolution of the wedding industry in the United States. Certainly, it is no surprise to learn that weddings have become big business. Yet, rather surprisingly, few scholars have attempted to explain how or why this $70 billion industry came to be. Painstakingly researched, Howard's book well illustrates how the "traditional" white wedding became an entrenched consumer rite during the twentieth century and how a massive industry grew up around it.

Conceivably, the book could have been organized chronologically, with chapters devoted to wedding culture during the Depression, the Cold War, the Sixties, etc. Instead, Howard chooses a more creative and more illuminating structure: she organizes her chapters around the chronology of the wedding process itself, from the initial steps of choosing rings to later decisions, like the hiring of a bridal consultant and the selection of the proper catering venue. Essentially, then, each chapter constitutes a mini-history of some element of the wedding industry. This organizational structure works effectively to highlight the many types of businesses that are involved with the wedding process. Howard emphasizes not just the role played by mass retailers, but also the roles of smaller firms, and, perhaps most interestingly, "kitchen capitalists"—those individuals, often women, who labor in their homes to perform a range of services for the bride.

While Howard does a commendable job of bringing into focus these many players, at the same time, she does not lose sight of the bigger picture. Constantly, throughout the book, she grapples with a fundamental question: how did weddings—traditionally considered by most Americans to be a private institution if not also a sacred one—morph into the highly commercialized phenomenon that exists today?

As Howard expertly highlights, it was no easy task for businesses to supplant certain older wedding practices (which often held religious and ethnic significance) with newer ones that held more profit potential for them. Doing so required the creation of "invented traditions," to borrow historian Eric Hobsbawm's phrase. To make new practices (like diamond engagement rings and the groom's band) acceptable and desirable, the wedding industry needed to make them appear as if they were rooted in

CHILDREN OF DIVORCE

Most young people who have experienced divorce do not believe parents should stay together for the sake of the children, according to a survey by the family law organisation Resolution.

The poll found that 82% of those aged 14 to 22 who have endured family breakups would prefer their parents to part if they are unhappy. They said it was ultimately better that their parents had divorced, with one of those surveyed adding that children "will often realise, later on, that it was for the best."

Asked what advice they would give divorcing parents, another said: "Don't stay together for a child's sake, better to divorce than stay together for another few years and divorce on bad terms."

The survey, released before the latest annual divorce figures from the Office of National Statistics, show that children want greater involvement in decisions made during the divorce process. More than 60% of those polled felt their parents had not ensured they were part of the decision-making process in their separation or divorce.

Half of young people indicated they did not have any say as to which parent they would live with or where they would live. An overwhelming majority—88%—agreed it was important to make sure children do not feel like they have to choose between parents.

ancient customs. At the same time, the industry also sought to subtly encourage the public to jettison practices that were not conducive to growing their businesses—such as the bride wearing an heirloom ring or a handed-down dress.

Perhaps what's most remarkable about this story is the amazing success of the wedding industry in propagating, despite obstacles, a new and ever-changing mass vision of what the "traditional" American wedding should look like. At various historical junctures, the vitality of the industry theoretically could have weakened— but it didn't. Despite a critical shortage of diamonds and other raw materials in World War II, for instance, the relatively new practice of giving diamond engagement rings persevered, as did the buying of white wedding gowns, increasingly for one-time

Feelings of confusion and guilt are commonplace. About half admitted not understanding what was happening during their parents' separation or divorce, while 19% agreed that they sometimes felt like it was their fault.

Resolution's research suggested that many parents handle their separations well: 50% of young people agreed that their parents put their needs first.

In the survey, carried out by ComRes, 514 young people aged 14–22 with experience of parental divorce or separation from a long-term cohabiting relationship were interviewed.

The findings are released before the parliamentary launch of an online advice guide developed by Resolution for divorcing parents to help manage relationships with their children and with each other.

When asked what they would most like to have changed about a divorce, 31% of young people said they would have liked their parents not to criticise each other in front of them; 30% said they would have liked their parents to understand what it felt like to be in the middle of the process.

"Children of Divorce: 82% Rather Parents Separate Than 'Stay for the Kids,'" by Owen Bowcott, Guardian News and Media Limited, November 22, 2015.

usage. In the late 1960s and early 1970s, the industry, in part by making some changes, also withstood criticisms by feminists that it (along with the marriage institution itself) exploited women. Today, as Howard's last chapter discusses, the wedding industry is still vibrant, in part because it is continually being reinvented.

It is interesting to contemplate (as Howard does) the degree to which consumers had the power to accept or reject the wedding industry's "strategies of enticement," to borrow William Leach's term. Howard insists, "Women, who were understood to be the main consumers of wedding-related goods and services, were not mere victims of advertising and merchandising campaigns, nor did they simply accept wedding industry advice uncritically" (p. 5). In one example of a failed "invented tradition," the male engagement ring never caught on, in part because it was unable to transcend contemporary gender mores. Howard also emphasizes the ways in which women, not just men, historically have been involved in marketing wedding products and services.

Finally, it is worthy to note that, in many ways, the act of consumption (not just production) can be construed as an act of marketing. The famous marketing guru Philip Kotler once wrote, "Buyers are Marketers, too." While Howard seems to implicitly recognize this (as she does spend some time detailing how consumers participated in the industry's transformation), she readily acknowledges that her book focuses on the "producers" in the story. This angle, though, actually works very well to illuminate many aspects of the development of the wedding industry that previously have not been closely examined.

Well-written and engaging, *Brides Inc.* is a welcome addition to the fields of twentieth-century business as well as cultural history.

> "*When men recognize biological
> paternity, they view their children
> as part of their own bodies and
> see that they, too, have a role
> in reproduction.*"

The Legitimacy or Illegitimacy of Children Impacts the Role of Marriage

Mara D. Giles

In the following viewpoint, Mara D. Giles examines ideas regarding legitimacy and illegitimacy of human offspring, following an evolutionary theory. Marriage is proposed as a cultural solution to fatherhood and perhaps the development of patriarchy in societies. Mara D. Giles is a scholarly researcher. Nebraska Anthropologist *is a peer-reviewed publication of the University of Nebraska-Lincoln AnthroGroup.*

As you read, consider the following questions:

1. Who is the intended audience for this viewpoint?
2. What are some theories of legitimacy and illegitimacy offered by the author?
3. What types of marriages does the viewpoint use as its focus?

"A Tri-Cultural Look at Legitimacy and Illegitimacy Using an Evolutionary Model," by Mara D. Giles, Digital Commons@University of Nebraska-Lincoln, *Nebraska Anthropologist* Vol. 19 (2003-2004). Reprinted by permission.

The concepts of legitimacy and illegitimacy are prevalent cross-culturally, whether one examines them in a matrilineal society, a patrilineal one, or a modem state system. We use the terms legitimate and illegitimate with an intuitive understanding of the definition; yet how complete is that insight? Teichman (1978: 54) provides a broad definition of illegitimacy that helps understanding:

> An illegitimate child is one whose conception and birth did not take place according to the rules which, in its parents' community, govern reproduction.

within the framework of Engles's evolutionary model of the creation of fatherhood leading to the concept of legitimacy.

Hendrix (1996: 6) argues that marriage is a function of the father-child. But in order to get a clearer idea of what illegitimacy is, one needs to consider those rules: what are they? Are they similar in different societies or do cultures have widely varying rules pertaining to illegitimacy?

In this study, the notions of legitimacy and illegitimacy will be examined in three distinct cultures: the Trobriand Islanders who are a matrilineal society, the Nuer who are a patrilineage, and England, a modem state system. Additionally, the impact of fatherhood, marriage, children's resource-use rights and a child's socially accepted inclusion into its society will be investigated with regards to legitimacy and illegitimacy in the aforementioned groups. This analysis will be placed bond in order to "[specify] the father's claim over the child and his obligations to it." O'Brien (1981) also makes the argument that paternity creates "a right to a child." There is a link then between fatherhood and marriage. Using Engles's evolutionary theory Hendrix (1996) states that when men recognize biological paternity, they view their children as part of their own bodies and see that they, too, have a role in reproduction. This in turn leads to the creation of fatherhood, so men will invest in the child by contributing resources to it and its mother. This is not as direct an involvement in rearing a child as the mother has with pregnancy and nursing, but it does provide the mother with safety and nourishment, which she passes on to the offspring. Resulting from the decision to make an investment of energy and resources in the mother and child, men want to make sure it is their own offspring in which they are investing. Paternity assurance is more difficult to determine when a woman has more than one male sexual partner and a man may be less willing to impart his resources to her if there is the chance that he is helping her to raise another man's child, for in essence this would mean that he is not really a part of the procreative process and is only being used as a material provider. Marriage stems, in part, from this new role of fatherhood and the passing of resources to the mother and her child. O'Brien (1981) adds that the control men have over the resources they provide to a mother and her child gave rise to sexual inequality and men's control over women and their children which helped to institutionalize marriage. Hendrix (1996) supports this by stating that men circumvented women and enhanced their role of father by claiming that without their direct support of the mother through provisioning she would not be able to properly or fully care for her child, thus reducing the woman's function to mere carrier of the child. Therefore the father's role evolved into one of supreme value. In other words, as a result of the control of the distribution of resources to women and their children, men established control over the sexuality of women in order to reduce the chances of their supporting other men's children. The main way to do this was through the invention of monandrous marriage: the socially recognized union of a woman to one man (Hendrix 1996). In the case of matrilineal societies, it is the mother's brother who has the role of social father: he is the child's link to the rest of the community, acting as teacher, guardian, and guide. Although in these societies there seems to be less restriction regarding women's sexuality, there are still rules pertaining to the distribution of resources to men's sister's offspring, as well as the presence of monandry. This will be illustrated subsequently in the paper by a look at the Trobriand Islanders. Though there are exceptions of polyandry as well, they are too rare to be considered for these purposes. These exceptions are often ecological adaptations that, given another option, would not be observed in their society. For instance, the Inuit have practiced ecologically based polyandry. Because the harsh environment in which they live made survival of a woman and her children difficult, it sometimes took more than one man pulling in resources to supply a household. Both men would have sexual access to the woman, but the amount of conflict that created made that type of union both unstable and less than ideal. When the resources of both men were no longer needed, or when the conflict led to violence, the polyandrous situation dissolved immediately (Balikci 1970).

A socially acknowledged union is important because it announces the claim a man has to a specific woman and the offspring they produce. Men use marriage to legally or socially lay claim to their children because they put in effort and resources into their maintenance. Inheritance becomes a factor to keep the link between child and social father known. Whether the inheritance is in the form of wealth, land, or status, what results is the recognition that the child is the legitimate child of said father because it was the product of the socially acknowledged union.

But what is socially acceptable marriage? Another way of asking this is do all marriages create legitimate offspring? For as Teichman (1978: 53) writes,

> From the fact that the children of a forbidden sexual union are illegitimate, it does not follow that children of a sanctioned sexual union must necessarily be legitimate.

The answer lies in the intrinsic link between resource control and who has legitimate access to those resources. Kin, meaning direct descendants (offspring) and close relatives (siblings), of the distributors of resources are the first group to have legitimate access to those resources because of their close social and biological bonds to the distributor. The next legitimate group regarding resource-use rights is those living endogamously. Here endogamy means people living in the same region, or belonging to the same culture, race, religion, class, or the like. This is the beginning of the classification of people and the existence of status (those who belong) and statuslessness (those who do not belong); in other words, those who have legitimate access to the wealth or status because of inclusion and those who do not because of their exclusion from the group to which the distributor of resources belongs. Some may argue that there are societies that have exogamous marriages and still produce legitimate children, but there are cultural adaptations that allow for these circumstances. Consider the Nuer and their capture of Dinka children. The abducted Dinka is considered at the very least to be the child of the captor and if adopted by the captor then the Dinka belongs to the father's lineage. If the Dinka is not adopted then he "attaches himself to his wife's people or to the people who have married his sister or daughter" (Evans-Pritchard 1951: 20) and his children, "having no lineage on the father's side, seek affiliation to the mother's lineage" (Evans-Pritchard 1951: 25). So it is that the members of the captor's household may not marry the captured Dinka and if he is adopted he may not marry any girl from his Nuer pater's lineage. Conversely if he is not adopted, then he may marry a girl from his captor's lineage because he does not legally belong to it. Thus while the Nuer practice "clan exogamy" (Evans- Pritchard 1951: 29) they still look for other Nuer, or people assimilated into Nuer culture. Therefore it is still a cultural endogamy, falling into the description of endogamous marriage just presented.

Additionally marriage, when used as a distributive force of wealth, is another way to create status and statuslessness, thus legitimacy and illegitimacy. Recall that socially accepted marriage is not only a way to claim rights over women's reproduction but to claim rights over the children produced. The advantage for a man is not only to be a part of the reproductive process but also to have someone to inherit from him and to continue his line, whether socially or biologically, acknowledging the less obvious link of child to social father. This is the case whether it is the mother's brother who has the important role of socializing the child in the Trobriand Islander's and other matrilineal societies, or the pater in the Nuer and similar patrilineages, or the patriarch in the English or other dowry-based household. This passing of resources gives a man a sense of contribution to the well-being of the child in his care. It acknowledges the inclusion of the child into his lineage or family as well as announces to the community the man's responsibility to socially prepare the child for its own role in society. All of this also resonates the urge for a man's self-continuity and his connection to procreation, whether through direct or inclusive fitness. The advantage for the child of having a man claim rights over him or her is to have someone from whom the child can inherit and to benefit his or her potential children. For instance, in lineage systems where resources belong to a corporate descent group and cannot be directly devolved, the use of the resources, such as land, can be passed on (Goody 1976). Fathers and lineages that have worked hard to socially establish themselves by increasing their wealth have higher status, thus pass on a greater right to use the land to their children (Weiner 1979) or more control over who uses what part of the land. By contrast, inheritance systems that have personal property pass the land and capital directly to children. Men that have worked harder to make capital gains have more wealth to impart to their offspring (Goody 1976). Thus in either type of system, claiming a right to a child incites that child to claim use of land or inheritance of assets from the father.

Legitimacy pertains to only certain children being able to lay claim on the father though. Because resources are limited to a certain extent in all societies, accordingly, families want to retain as much control over the land and material goods and status as possible. Therefore creating endogamous classifications keeps those resources closer to the distributor by stating only those who fall into his particular category can inherit available wealth. Socially acceptable marriage is a derivative of endogamous classifications because marrying endogamously retains the wealth in a particular group. Since both a child's parents belong to the endogamous group, so does the child, thus it is considered a legitimate inheritor. Consider an example,

In early times the Church always demanded that the parties to a Christian marriage both be Christians. Marriages of Christians to Jews or infidels were illegal… Any children of such a union would of course be illegitimate (Teichman 1978: 35).

Although exogamous unions, whether they are inter-religious, inter-caste, inter- racial, etc. do take place, as stated above they are often considered socially illegal and the products of such unions are not recognized as legitimate, i.e. within the rules. Prescribing endogamous marriages helps to prevent mixing of groups and to reduce illegitimacy. One defense for this way of thinking may have been the difficulties in trying to decide to which group did the child belong, for being of both groups it was a "misfit in the status system" (Hendrix 1996: 29). But in reality, these rules are used "to organize and limit claims against the family estate" (Hendrix 1996: 84) or the group to which the distributor of resources belongs. Consequently, legitimacy is a status of marriage, but not just any type of marriage. It is the status of the socially acceptable marriage and is a way to create rules of inclusion and exclusion for resource and status distribution.

Illegitimacy of children in its simplest form is a child born of incest. But incest as viewed in our culture, i.e. sexual relationships (and children born thereof) between near-related kin or persons fulfilling those roles, is not so viewed in all cultures. Near-relatedness begins with the nuclear family: parent-child and sibling-sibling, and spreads out from there to the next most closely blood-related family members. Most societies do in fact forbid sexual intercourse between relatives in the nuclear family (Murdock 1965). While some cultures, such as our own, extend the prohibition to non-genetically related individuals performing roles of the nuclear family, such as step-parents and stepsiblings, other societies sanction some biologically incestuous sexual relationships because they are not socially incestuous. For example, Montague (1971) noted that the Trobriand Islanders do acknowledge sister-brother, mother-son, and father-daughter incest. But the latter is often overlooked because technically the father is of a different lineage than the daughter and is not considered either social or biological incest. Any offspring resulting from such a union are not classified as illegitimate solely based on the father-daughter relationship. (The product child may be illegitimate for other reasons though.) On the other hand, mother-son and sister-brother incest will always produce illegitimate offspring. These relationships are taboo because since both parties of the union belong to the same lineage, it is social incest.

For the Trobriand Islanders, all forms of illegitimacy stem directly from the incest taboo. Although Malinowski reported that the Trobriand Islanders did not understand the connection between sexual intercourse and pregnancy, the reality is that they have a very complex mythological explanation for pregnancy to accommodate their cultural forms of inclusion and exclusion (Montague 1971). Since the Trobrianders are a matrilineal people, lineage passes through the mother, but rank and land-use rights pass through the father. However this society also practices avunculocality. The maternal uncle is socially responsible for the children of his sister; as Weiner (1979: 329) explains: "the avuncular relationship replaced the paternal, and the authority of descent superceded the primacy of the nuclear family." In order to understand the Trobrianders' sense of illegitimacy, we must first understand the relationship between sister and brother. Because of the nature of the matrilineal-avuncular relationship, a brother and sister have a strong social bond with one another that leads to physical proximity and emotional closeness. In context of child rearing they are much like husband and wife. However, because of the strict incest taboo between sister and brother they must perform avoidance behaviors constantly.

If an unmarried Trobriand woman gives birth to a child, any married couple that lacks or desires a child can adopt it. If there is no one else to adopt the infant the responsibility falls upon the mother's brother since he is also the child's main male authority figure. However, by adopting it, this indicates that the child's maternal uncle is also its father. But since the infant's mother is also the uncle's sister, this implies incest, albeit social incest. However, this is taboo and thus the child would remain illegitimate. Yet Malinowski had claimed that the Trobrianders had no concept of the link between sex and procreation so why should this concept of illegitimacy exist? Montague (1971: 365) refutes this idea arguing that "[t]he Trobriand Islanders are, and apparently always have been, fully aware of the correlation between sexual intercourse and pregnancy." The Trobrianders believe in spirits of ancestors that desire to reincarnate themselves, and so they take on a child-spirit form called a waiwaia that inserts itself into the woman through her head or vagina, the latter of which can be opened in ways other than sexual intercourse (Montague 1971). Once the waiwaia is housed in the woman's body, it needs the menstrual blood for nourishment. A man's semen, but not necessarily the husband's, is needed to keep the blood from flowing out of the mother's womb. The waiwaia enters this substance and uses it to take on physicality, which is then molded into human form by the husband's proximity to the mother during pregnancy. When the infant is born, the husband of the woman legitimizes the child through the ritual "exchanges of objects...which establishes a relationship of equality" (Montague 1971: 361) between the husband as father and the child. This act gives the child rank and if the child is a son, the use of the lineage's land, a uniquely human employment. At this point rank becomes very complex and since inter-rank-class unions are possible because legitimization is still consummated by the husband (Montague 1971), I will not examine the various rank systems.

Thus the two most basic forms of Trobriand child legitimacy are attained through a husband. The first form of legitimization is that a husband, in passing land use and possession rights to a child, classifies it as legitimately human as opposed to animal, for animals do not own or work land as humans do. The second form of legitimization is that the presence of a husband, and hence a man from a different lineage than the mother, makes a child a culturally acceptable human, implying that the child is not the. product of incest, at least social or terminological incest. Thus we see that marriage is important because it symbolizes the legitimacy of the child produced.

Leaving the genetic and psychological effects of incest aside, why should products of incest be socially problematic? What would lead them to be illegitimate? For one thing, there is the complex matter of classification: who is this individual in relation to its kin? With lineage systems in particular, a confusion of this sort would make it difficult to categorize the child into its separate marriageable and non-marriageable groups. In societies where there are already limited numbers of marriageable people to choose from, it is necessary to classify people properly in order to avoid incestuous unions, whether they are biologically or socially incestuous. For another thing, there is the issue of breaking the incest taboo that exists in the society, for as noted above, these definitely exist for the nuclear family in most societies, if not for all classificatory mothers, daughters, fathers, and sons. By virtue of the fact that the taboo, i.e. cultural law, would have been broken would make the offspring of the union illegitimate because of its illegality. Marriage then seems to be an acceptable and effective solution for controlling this form of illegitimacy, for it gives people culturally appropriate sexual access to one another in order to produce children that can be classified into marriageable and non-marriageable groups themselves.

The Nuer also abide by an incest taboo to determine legitimacy and illegitimacy and have very strict rules as to who is non-marriageable based on both social and biological incest. These include,

> the clan kinship of the common spear; the buth kinship of collateral lineage an of adoption; uterine kinship; kinship through the genitor; the kinship of cognation; kinship which the birth of a child creates between affines; the kinship acknowledged by acceptance of bridewealth; and the kinship by analogy of the age-set (Evans-Pritchard 1951: 34).

These kinships are the result of the link to the paternal line as well as the maternal. Since the Trobriand Islanders have a matrilineal system, they are concerned with incest and illegitimacy only in relation to the mother's line. But the Nuer, being a patrilineal society, understand that socio-biological link of father to child in addition to the mother's connection. Consequently their non-marriageable rules become more intricate since more factors are involved, and this in terms of illegitimacy makes "social control of sex and reproduction...more repressive" (Hendrix 1996: 77). So if a Nuer child is born out of wedlock, not only is it using resources that the mother's family needs compensated by the genitor's lineage, but it also has not been classified into its framework of interlineage relationships (Evans-Pritchard 1951) and its marriageable and non-marriageable categories to avoid incest. For this reason, although premarital sex is not frowned upon, premarital birth is.

Additionally, the Nuer are a brideprice society and though they comprehend paternity certainty and have land-use rights and status inheritance, children are also valued as resources themselves. To understand then how the Nuer determine child legitimacy, one must look at the objectives brideprice accomplishes. Firstly, it legitimizes the marriage union as proof that it is not incestuous; secondly, it creates affinal bonds that are important for alliance as well as for kinship categorization of marriageable and non-marriageable; thirdly, it provides a family with economic replacement of female labor. Through payment of brideprice, children are included in their father's lineage, but as Evans-Pritchard (1951: 98) explains it does not necessarily have to be the biological father that makes a claim on a child for "[t]he man in whose name the cattle were paid is always their pater, the legal or lineage father, whether he is their genitor or not." So when a Nuer woman has a baby out of wedlock, it is still cared for and belongs to her lineage until a man pays her brideprice and legitimizes her child by making a claim on it, allowing the child then to make claims back on him (Hendrix 1996). However, if the legal husband, the one who paid the brideprice, dies and his widow becomes sexually involved with a man not of her dead husband's lineage, any children she bears to the lover are still born to her husband's lineage unless the lover selects to pay the brideprice to wed her and claim his children legally. Thus it is again through the transaction of marriage that rights of inclusion over a child are claimed and that enables a child to inherit resources from its father.

Davis (1939a : 224) states that "[a] universal rule is that the illegitimate child does not acquire full membership in the family group or family line of his parent" because it is not the product of the socially sanctioned union and not legally bound to the lineally significant parent. Since in the majority of all societies it is the woman who is economically dependant on her husband for reasons already shown, inheritance is passed down from the father to the child, or in the case of matrilineal systems from the mother's brother to the child. But an illegitimate child, not being a full member of a family and thus not a legal successor of a social father also cannot inherit from him. Davis puts this very succinctly:

> [s]ince the child does not descend from the father and does not bear his name, it follows that the father's family...will scarcely wish, as a family, to see property inherited by a filius nullius... thus the rule of noninheritance is a corollary of the rule of nondescent, both being part and parcel of the reproductive structure. (1939a : 225)

This is especially true as societies become more highly stratified, for as increase of inheritance of wealth and status are achievements of power and social dominance, there will b e less inclination by families to share that power with illegal members of their group.

In hierarchical societies like England, "[l]egitimacy is relative to the legal system" (Teichman 1978: 3) which makes both illegitimacy and legitimacy legal statuses based on legal marriage. According to English law, a legal marriage is one that is not voidable, where void means the law does not acknowledge the marriage. For example, a void marriage in England would be a polygynous union for the law does not recognize that as a legal form of marriage and any children born to such a union would be illegitimate.

Because of the nature of the dowry system described by Goody (1976), English marriages are monogamous. The fact that there is land tenure means there are limited resources to pass on to offspring. The combination of monogamy and scarcity of assets leads to fewer descendants and less spreading of wealth. Goody (1976) discusses the idea of diverging devolution in which both sons and daughters received inheritance to keep them at their level in the hierarchy and thus in the socially dominant positions. (For those families that were poor this would not have mattered much, but laws are often written to benefit those who have wealth and power to lose.) In monogamy, the birth or survival of sons is not guaranteed so wealth is often passed to a daughter. Originally the property remained her father's until she married when it passed to her husband. "In law, in lineage, and in matters having to do with property, a woman, until modem times, was a kind of nullity" (Teichman 1978: 83). As this was the case, children also did not legally belong to the mother since

> [t]he rearing of children is a task which requires a considerable amount of money and cannot be successfully undertaken by an individual who is herself in a state of financial dependence (Teichman 1978: 18).

Reasons for this non-legal status of women had to do with the power to pass on inheritance and retain status and power in the man's name, whether the father or the husband. However, as a result of the stratified society, upper class women were able to voice their political and social opinions more freely because of the financial contributions they made to their marriage. Resulting from this, over the centuries there were legal changes in which women were allowed to own property and petition for divorce on their own. This implies that they were financially less dependent on their husbands than previously and could support themselves without their husbands' capital assistance. In 1839 legislation was passed that legally recognized women as mothers and guardians of their own children (Teichman 1978), because of the ability for them to own property and wealth and maintain their children themselves.

However, this new law pertained to legitimate children only. Because the illegitimate child was not born under a legal contract and therefore had no legal father, it was considered filius nullius, no-one's child. In fact, as late as 1958 English law stated "only a man can legitimate a child" (Teichman 1978: 33). An illegitimate child of the wealthy could be cared for by its mother and her family or maintained by its father because of the available resources. But this in itself did not legitimate it. And what of the poor, who had no means to support their illegitimate children? In pre-Roman times through the 16th century, the illegitimate child was put to death and sometimes the mother was too, especially if the illegitimacy was the result of adultery. In the 1600s the church began to care for many of the illegitimate children, using them as labor resources. But when the church "began to feel overburdened by the large number of illegitimate in [its] care" (Teichman 1978: 25), it looked for a way to get financial help from the putative fathers. This was not always successful and in the 1800s the parish grew tired of the work involved in maintaining illegitimate children and passed the burden on to the mother. This action changed the way women were viewed in society because until this time "unmarried mothers had no legal rights at all in regard to their children" (Teichman 1978: 28) and now with the church demanding the responsibility be removed from it and put on the woman, there was the idea that an illegitimate child could even have a parent: the mother. Removing the label of filius nullius from the child changed the status of women from null to parents, thereby opening the door for them to petition for rights of custody and adoption of their own offspring born out of wedlock. As already stated, wealthier families did not have such difficulties for they had resources to provide. But poor women were limited in their options and severely stigmatized until they too could own property and participate in the workforce.

Adoption, not for the sake of finding an heir, but to remove the shame of illegitimacy posed a problem for it was one thing to maintain an illegitimate child and quite another to legalize it. Several Adoption Acts from the first part of the 20th century gave an adopted child the same rights as a legitimate child (Teichman 1978).

While this was acceptable when a man (whether the biological father or not) adopted a child because of his long-standing legal power and tradition to pass on inheritance, there was fear amongst lawmakers that illegitimacy would be abolished should women be allowed to adopt their illegitimate offspring for the purpose of legitimization, even if they had the financial freedom to do so. What lawmakers objected to was the potential disappearance of the institution of marriage, for if women could legitimize their own children born out of a sanctioned union, why have marriage to begin with? The segregation of legitimate and illegitimate was necessary in order to draw a distinct line between the legal and the illegal. This generated another whole set of arguments trying to maintain an ideology of legitimacy. If women could now pass inheritance to their own offspring, then that potentially made marriage obsolete. But lawmakers, as voices of the powerful in society, believed the sanctity of marriage and of the family were what separated the moral from the immoral, and they used these ideas to define legitimacy and illegitimacy instead. Today the debate regarding illegitimacy in many modem state systems is an issue of immorality over illegality.

But if at this point marriage is no longer a criterion for legitimacy, at least in some places, what then creates the illegitimate? Malinowski's Principle of Legitimacy states,

> No child shall be brought into the world without a man, and one man, assuming the role of sociological father...the male link between a child and the rest of the community (Malinowski, 1930: 134).

Kingsley Davis (1939a) also asserts that a father is paramount for giving full social status to the child and its mother. But as just indicated, legal adoption of a child by an unmarried woman is possible for legitimization in the modem state society. Teichman (1978) introduces the concept of the family, whatever the societal concept may be, as criteria for inclusion or exclusion. As we saw with the Trobriand Islanders, descent and thus family was traced back through the mother's lineage. The Nuer trace descent patrilineally, which defines the family. England, too, traces family through males, the traditional guardians of "names, property-rights and power" (Teichman 1978: 62). In essence then, an illegitimate child is excluded from the family as a social unit, not allowed to partake of the social advantages of being included. Teichman herself argues against this point saying this is not enough of a definition for illegitimacy, but taking the three facets together, fatherhood, marriage, and family and all the rewards stemming from them, we see from where the concept of illegitimacy came.

We still return to the issue of adoption by women in modern state societies. As has been demonstrated, it is with the increase of the status and power of women that the concept of illegitimacy comes into question. Indeed punitive measures against transgressors become more egalitarian in societies where women have more power, but they never disappear (Hendrix 1996). But as women are able to take more control over their lives, they become less dependent on men for their existence, and so do their children from a financial perspective. To be sure the combination of resource scarcity and paternity certainty created marriage, and while fatherhood, marriage, and the family are cross-cultural determinants for legitimacy and illegitimacy, if those commonalities are not necessary when women are financially independent, what answers for the persistence of legitimacy and illegitimacy?

Perhaps all the rules for deterring illegitimacy, such as early marital age for girls in some societies, or severe punitive action taken against the individuals for their indiscretion, or even the ability of women to adopt their own child are adaptive responses to a bigger picture. Perhaps the ultimate cause for having the separation between the legitimate and the illegitimate is a way to reduce the number of births so resources are not used so quickly. For by limiting the number of children born within a framework of rules, the number of people claiming resource-use rights is also limited. Early marital age for girls generally results in fewer illegitimate births. Punishment of offenders deters many others from having illegitimate children. Adoption of children by their own mothers is a solid legal solution making the illegitimate legitimate, and if the mothers are financially responsible for their offspring they may be less likely to have other children unless they can maintain them. Perhaps then the concept of illegitimacy is a method of population control used worldwide.

Or perhaps it is that need that most people have to feel included in the procreative process. Many men, who are already greatly removed from it, desire to find ways to be a part of it and ensure their social connection to the child. We have seen this with the Trobriand Islanders whose concept of fatherhood is social and not completely biological, and with the Nuer, who value children as resources and continuance of lineages, and with the English, who found that when men were no longer the proverbial breadwinners they advocated still for marriage so they could remain connected socially and biologically to their children. So perhaps the concept of legitimacy is the result of a given man acknowledging his care for a child as a means to demonstrate his inclusion in that child's, and thus his society's and life's, existence. Or perhaps it is as Hendrix (1996) claimed, a power issue men enjoyed having over the sexuality of women and the children they produced, and they are loath to give that up.

Whatever the ultimate causes for illegitimacy are, whether resource distribution, fatherhood, or family, surely marriage is the defining factor. In all three societies at which were looked, marriage was used as the determinant of legitimacy and the exclusion of the illegitimate from perquisites of the legally sanctioned union. Having just looked at three cultures, though vastly different, one might question the assertion that marriage and legitimacy of children go hand in hand. But marriage is a cross-cultural phenomenon, as are legitimacy and illegitimacy.

References Cited

Balikci, Asen, 1989 *The Netsilik Eskimo*. Waveland Press, Inc, Prospect Heights.

Bell, Duran, 1997 Defining Marriage and Legitimacy. *Current Anthropology* 38(2):237-253.

Davis, Kingsley, 1939a The Forms of Illegitimacy. *Social Forces* 18(1):77-89, 114. 1939b Illegitimacy and the Social Structure. *The American Journal of Sociology* 45(2):215-233.

Evans-Pritchard, Edward E, 1951 *Kinship and Marriage Among the Nuer*. Oxford University Press, London.

Goody, Jack, 1976 *Production and Reproduction: A Comparative Study of the Domestic Domain*. Cambridge University Press, Cambridge.

Hendrix, Lewellyn, 1996 *Illegitimacy and Social Structures: Cross-Cultural Perspectives on Nonmarital Birth*. Bergin and Garvey, Westport.

Malinowski, Bronislaw, 1930 Parenthood: The Basis of Social Structure. In *The New Generation: the Intimate Problems of Modern Parents and Children*, edited by Victor F. Calverton and Samuel D. Schmalhausen. St. Martin's Press, New York. 1962 *Sex, Culture, and Myth*. Harcourt and Brace, New York.

Montague, Susan, 1971 Trobriand Kinship and the Virgin Birth Controversy. *Man* 6(3):353- 368.

Murdock, George P., 1965 *Social Structure*. The Free Press, New York.

O'Brien, Mary, 1981 *The Politics of Reproduction*. Routledge and Kegan Paul, Boston.

Pasternak, Burton, Carol R. Ember, and Melvin Ember. 1997 *Sex, Gender, and Kinship: A Cross-Cultural Perspective*. Prentice-Hall, New Jersey.

Teichman, Jenny, 1978 *The Meaning of Illegitimacy*. Englehardt Books, Cambridge. 1982 *Illegitimacy: An Examination of Bastardy*. Cornell University Press, Ithaca.

Weiner, A., 1979 Trobriand Kinship from Another View: The Reproductive Power of Women and Men. *Man* 14(2):328- 348.

> *"Most in the US harbor both implicit and explicit biases against interracial couples. These biases were quite robust, showing up among those who had had close personal contact with interracial couples."*

Americans Are More Biased Against Interracial Couples Than They Want to Admit

Allison Skinner

In the following viewpoint, Allison Skinner details her study on interracial marriage and dating in the United States, looking for both explicit and implicit bias in attitudes concerning interracial relationships. The study was designed to indicate how widespread negative attitudes were toward interracial couples 50 years after the abolition of miscegenation laws. Allison Skinner is a social psychologist and assistant professor of psychology at the University of Georgia.

"How Do Americans Really Feel About Interracial Couples?" by Allison Skinner, The Conversation, July 5, 2018. https://theconversation.com/how-do-americans-really-feel -about-interracial-couples-99173. Licensed under CC BY-ND 4.0 International.

As you read, consider the following questions:

1. How does each race feel about interracial marriage, according to the author?
2. What are explicit and implicit bias?
3. According to the viewpoint, is there proof that attitudes are changing?

According to the most recent US census, approximately 15 percent of all newlywed couples are interracial. More interracial relationships are also appearing in the media—on television, in film and in advertising.

These trends suggest that great strides have been made in the roughly 50 years since the Supreme Court struck down anti-miscegenation laws.

But as a psychologist who studies racial attitudes, I suspected that attitudes toward interracial couples may not be as positive as they seem. My previous work had provided some evidence of bias against interracial couples. But I wanted to know how widespread that bias really is.

What Does Each Race Think?

To answer this question, my collaborator James Rae and I recruited participants from throughout the US to examine implicit and explicit attitudes toward black-white interracial couples.

Psychologists typically differentiate between explicit biases— which are controlled and deliberate—and implicit biases, which are automatically activated and tend to be difficult to control.

So someone who plainly states that people of different races shouldn't be together would be demonstrating evidence of explicit bias. But someone who reflexively thinks that interracial couples would be less responsible tenants or more likely to default on a loan would be showing evidence of implicit bias.

In this case, we assessed explicit biases by simply asking participants how they felt about same-race and interracial couples.

We assessed implicit biases using something called the implicit association test, which requires participants to quickly categorize same-race and interracial couples with positive words, like "happiness" and "love," and negative words, like "pain" and "war." If it takes participants longer to categorize interracial couples with positive words, it's evidence that they likely possess implicit biases against interracial couples.

MARRIAGE TRENDS BY RACE-ETHNICITY AND NATIVITY

Women's potential eligibility for spousal and survivor benefits based on their marital history varies significantly by race and ethnicity. For example, in 2009, 34 percent of black women aged 50–59 had marital histories that made them ineligible for spousal or survivor benefits, compared with 14 percent of non-Hispanic white women and 17 percent of Hispanic women of the same age.

The proportion of women aged 40 to 59 without qualifying marriages for spousal and survivor benefits increased between 1990 and 2009, particularly among black women. For example, 41 percent of black women age 40 to 49 lacked a qualifying marriage in 2009, compared to 20 percent of white women, a difference of 21 percentage points. In 1990, the difference was about 13 percentage points (24 percent black and 11 percent white). This widening gap is driven, in large part, by a higher proportion of black women who never marry among more recent cohorts.

Among Hispanic women, potential eligibility for spouse and survivor benefits based on marital history varies substantially by nativity. In 2009, more US-born Hispanic women lacked a qualifying marriage (21 percent for ages 50–59 and 28 percent ages 40–49) than foreign-born (14 percent for ages 50–59 and 13 percent ages 40–49). The composition of the Hispanic population is heterogeneous and has changed greatly from 1990 to 2009 with recent waves of immigration.

"Marriage Trends and Women's Benefits: Differences by Race-Ethnicity and Nativity," US Social Security Administration, February 2014.

In total, we recruited approximately 1,200 white people, over 250 black people and over 250 multiracial people to report their attitudes. We found that overall, white and black participants from across the US showed statistically significant biases against interracial couples on both the implicit measure and the explicit measure.

In contrast, participants who identified as multiracial showed no evidence of bias against interracial couples on either measure.

Although we cannot know for sure from our data, we believe that the lack of bias observed among multiracial participants may stem from the fact that they're the product of an interracial relationship. Then there's the reality of their own romantic relationships. Multiracial people have few romantic options that would not constitute an interracial relationship: Over 87 percent of multiracial participants in our sample reported having dated interracially.

Predicting Bias

We also wanted to know what might predict bias against interracial couples.

We anticipated that those who had previously been in an interracial romantic relationship—or were currently involved in one—would hold more positive attitudes.

For both white and black participants, this is precisely what we found. There was one catch: Black participants who had previously been in an interracial relationship were just as likely to harbor explicit biases as those who hadn't been in one.

Next, we wanted to test whether having close contact—in other words, spending quality time with interracial couples— was associated with positive attitudes toward interracial couples. Psychological evidence has shown that contact with members of other groups tends to reduce intergroup biases.

To get at this, we asked participants questions about how many interracial couples they knew and how much time they spent with them. We found that across all three racial groups, more interpersonal contact with interracial couples meant more positive implicit and explicit attitudes toward interracial couples.

Finally, we examined whether just being exposed to interracial couples—such as seeing them around in your community—would be associated with more positive attitudes toward interracial couples. Some have argued that exposure to interracial and other "mixed status" couples can serve as a catalyst to reduce biases.

Our results, however, showed no evidence of this.

In general, participants who reported more exposure to interracial couples in their local community reported no less bias than those who reported very little exposure to interracial couples. In fact, among multiracial participants, those who reported more exposure to interracial couples in their local community actually reported more explicit bias against interracial couples than those with less exposure.

The Outlook for the Future

According to polling data, only a small percentage of people in the US—9 percent—say that the rise in interracial marriage is a bad thing.

Yet our findings indicate that most in the US harbor both implicit and explicit biases against interracial couples. These biases were quite robust, showing up among those who had had close personal contact with interracial couples and even some who had once been involved in interracial romantic relationships.

The only ones who didn't show biases against interracial couples were multiracial people.

Nonetheless, in 2015, 14 percent of all babies born nationwide were mixed race or mixed ethnicity—nearly triple the rate in 1980. In Hawaii, the rate is 44 percent. So despite the persistence of bias against interracial couples, the number of multiracial people in the US will only continue to grow—which bodes well for interracial couples.

> *"Marriage is currently a crazy quilt*
> *of special privileges and goodies*
> *that everybody wants access to—*
> *unmarried people be damned. But*
> *marriage should confer neither*
> *special favors nor goodies from*
> *the state."*

Marriage Should Be Privatized

Max Borders

In the following viewpoint, Max Borders argues that the government should be kept out of the business of marriage. The author notes that several disparate groups agree, albeit for very different reasons, and contends that states should establish default civil unions as alternatives to private marriages. Max Borders is a former editor at the Foundation for Economic Freedom and author of The Social Singularity.

As you read, consider the following questions:

1. What two definitions of marriage does the author distinguish between?
2. According to the author, what might have solved the same-sex marriage debate?
3. What other areas could benefit from privatization, according to the viewpoint?

"On Privatizing Marriage," by Max Borders, Foundation for Economic Freedom, August 25, 2015. https://fee.org/articles/on-privatizing-marriage/. Licensed under CC BY-4.0 International.

The idea of marriage privatization is picking up steam. And it makes strange bedfellows.

There are old-school gay activists suspicious that state marriage is a way for politicians to socially engineer the family through the tax code. There are religious conservatives who are upset that a state institution seems to violate their sacred values. Don't forget the libertarians for whom "privatize it" is more a reflex than a product of reflection.

But they all agree: it would be a good idea to get the government out of the marriage business. Principle, it turns out, is pragmatic.

First, let's disentangle two meanings for one word that easily get confused. When we say "marriage," we might be referring to:

A. a commitment a couple enters into as a rite or acknowledgment within a religious institution or community group (private); or

B. a legal relationship that two people enter into, which the state currently licenses (public).

Now, the questions that follow are: Does the government need to be involved in A? The near-universal answer in the United States is no. But does the government need to be as involved as it is in B? Here's where the debate gets going.

I think the government can and should get out of B, and everyone will be better for it. This is what I mean by marriage privatization.

Some argue that marriage is "irreducibly public." For Jennifer Roback Morse, it has to do with the fate of children and families. For Shikha Dalmia, it has to do with the specter of increased government involvement, a reinflamed culture war, and a curious concern about religious institutions creating their own marriage laws.

First, let's consider the issue of children. According to Unmarried.org:

- 39.7 percent of all births are to unmarried women (Centers for Disease Control, 2007).

- Nearly 40 percent of heterosexual, unmarried American households include children (Child Protective Services, 2007).
- 41 percent of first births by unmarried women are to cohabiting partners (Larry Bumpass and Hsien-Hen Lu, 2000).

Does the law leave provisions for the children of the unmarried? Of course. So while state marriage might add some special sauce to your tax bill or to your benefits package, family court and family codes aren't likely to go anywhere, whatever we do with marriage. This is not a sociological argument about whether children have statistically better life prospects when they are brought up by two married parents. Nor is it a question about gender, sexuality, and parental roles. It's simply a response to the idea that marriage is "irreducibly public" due to having children. It is not. (I'll pass over the problem for this argument that some married couples never have children.)

Dalmia is also concerned that "true privatization would require more than just getting the government out of the marriage licensing and registration business. It would mean giving communities the authority to write their own marriage rules and enforce them on couples."

It's true. Couples, as a part of free religious association, might have to accept some definition of marriage as a condition of membership in a religious community. But, writes Dalmia, "This would mean letting Mormon marriages be governed by the Church of the Latter Day Saints codebook, Muslims by Koranic sharia, Hassids by the Old Testament, and gays by their own church or non-religious equivalent." And all of this is could be true up to a point.

But Dalmia overstates the case. Presumably, no religious organization would be able to set up codes that run counter to the civil and criminal laws in some jurisdiction. So if it were part of the Koranic sharia code to beat your wife for failure to wear the hijab at Costco, that rule would run afoul of laws against spousal abuse.

Mormon codes might sanction polygamy, but the state might have other ideas. So again, it's not clear what sort of magical protection state marriage conjures.

What about Dalmia's concern that in the absence of state marriage, "every aspect of a couple's relationship would have to be contractually worked out from scratch in advance"? Never mind that some people would see being able to work out the details of a contract governing their lives as a good thing (for one, it might prevent ugly divorce proceedings). There is no reason to think that all the functions normal, unmarried couples with children and property have in terms of recourse to "default" law would not still be available. Not only would simple legal templates for private marriage emerge, but states could establish default civil unions in the absence of couples pursuing private alternatives.

Indeed, if people did not like some default option—as they might not now—there would be better incentives for couples to anticipate the eventualities of marital life. People would have to settle questions involving cohabitation, property, and children just as they do for retirement and for death. Millions of gay couples had to do this prior to the Supreme Court's ruling on marriage equality. Millions of unmarried couples do it today. The difference is that there would be a set of private marriage choices in a layer atop the default, just as people may opt for private arbitration in lieu of government courts.

In the debates leading up to marriage equality, an eminently sensible proposal had been that even if you don't like the idea of hammering out a detailed contract with your spouse-to-be, simply changing the name of the entire statutory regime to "civil unions" would have gone a long way toward putting the whole gay-marriage debate to bed. The conservatives would have been able to say that, in terms of their sacred traditions and cultural community (as in A), "marriage" is between one man and one woman. Gay couples would have to find a church or institution that would marry them under A. But everybody would have some equal legal provision under the law to get all the benefits that accrue to people under B. You'd just have to call it a "civil union."

And that's fine as far as it goes.

But I like full privatization because "marriage" is currently a crazy quilt of special privileges and goodies that everybody wants access to—unmarried people be damned. But marriage should confer neither special favors nor goodies from the state. We can quibble about who is to be at the bedside of a dying loved one. Beyond that, marriage (under definition B) is mostly about equal access to government-granted privileges.

Not only does the idea that marriage is irreducibly public represent a failure of imagination with respect to robust common law, it also resembles arguments made against privatization in other areas, such as currency, education, and health care. Just because we can't always envision it doesn't make it impossible.

> *"Changing family patterns are not simply the result of financial instability. They reflect choices: Not everyone wants romantic partnership, and many singles see solo life as more conducive to flourishing and autonomy."*

Marriage Is Not for Everyone

Elizabeth Brake

In the following viewpoint, Elizabeth Brake argues that marriage—and even coupledom—should not be the default societal expectation. In fact, she contends, many people prefer to remain single. The author explores a variety of people who flourish on their own and who challenge the expectation that everyone wants a romantic sexual partnership. Elizabeth Brake is assistant professor of philosophy at Arizona State University. Her research focuses on marriage, sexuality, and procreative ethics.

As you read, consider the following questions:

1. By what year did married couples become a minority in the United States?
2. According to the viewpoint, for whom does marriage bring extra work?
3. What is the difference between asexual and aromantic?

"Single Doesn't Mean Being Lonely or Alone," by Elizabeth Brake, The Conversation, December 20, 2018. https://theconversation.com/single-doesnt-mean-being-lonely-or-alone-108665. Licensed under CC BY-ND 4.0.

As the holidays transition to the New Year, singles may face questions from friends and family: "When are you getting serious about dating?"

In many families, seasonal festivities draw lines between who's coupled and who's not. Romantic partners are invited to holiday meals, included in family photographs, and seen as potential life mates—while "mere" friends are not. These practices draw a line between relationships seen as significant—and those that aren't.

As I've argued in my research on the ethics and politics of the family, these practices reflect widespread assumptions. One is that everyone is seeking a romantic relationship. The second is more value-laden: living in a long-term romantic, sexual partnership is better than living without one. This fuels beliefs that those living solo are less happy, or lonelier, than couples.

These assumptions are so prevalent that they guide many social interactions. But research shows they're false.

Why More Americans Are Living Single

The truth is that more Americans are living unmarried and without a romantic partner. In 2005, the census for the first time recorded a majority of women living outside of marriage. Although, of course, some unmarried women have romantic partners.

In 2010, married couples became a minority in the United States. The percentage of unmarried adults is at an all-time high, with more young adults choosing to live unmarried and without a romantic partner.

Personal finances likely play a role in such choices. Millennials are worse off than earlier generations. There is a proven connection between economic resources and marriage rates—what legal scholar Linda McClain calls "the other marriage equality problem." Lower incomes correlate with lower rates of marriage.

But changing family patterns are not simply the result of financial instability. They reflect choices: Not everyone wants romantic partnership, and many singles see solo life as more conducive to flourishing and autonomy.

Single by Choice

As I show in my book *Minimizing Marriage*, people have many different political or ethical reasons for preferring singlehood.

Some women become single mothers by choice. As sociologist Arlie Hochschild has argued, marriage brings extra work for women, making it less attractive than single life for some.

For other people, being single is simply a relationship preference or even an orientation. For example, there are those, referred to as "asexuals" and "aromantics," who lack interest in sexual and romantic relationships.

Who Are Asexuals and Aromantics?

Data from a 1994 British survey of more than 18,000 people showed 1 percent of the respondents to be asexual. Because asexuality is still little-known, some asexuals might not identify as such. And so, it's possible that the true numbers could be higher.

Asexuals are people who do not feel sexual attraction. Asexuality is not simply the behavior of abstaining from sex, but an orientation. Just as straight people feel sexual attraction to members of a different sex, and gays and lesbians feel attraction to members of the same sex, asexuals simply do not feel sexual attraction. Asexuals can have romantic feelings, wanting a life partner to share intimate moments with and even cuddle—but without sexual feelings.

But some asexuals are also aromantic, that is, not interested in romantic relationships. Like asexuality, aromanticism is an orientation. Aromantics may have sexual feelings or be asexual, but they do not have romantic feelings. Both asexuals and aromantics face a lack of understanding.

Angela Chen, a journalist writing a book about asexuality, reports that her asexual interview subjects suffered from a lack of information about asexuality. As they failed to develop sexual attractions during puberty—while their classmates did—they asked themselves, "Am I normal? Is something wrong with me?"

But while asexuality is sometimes misunderstood as a medical disorder, there are many differences between an asexual orientation and a medical disorder causing a low sex drive. When asexuals are treated as "abnormal" by doctors or therapists, it does them a disservice.

Since the early 2000s, asexuals have exchanged ideas and organized through online groups. One such group, the Asexual Visibility and Education Network, for example, promotes the understanding that lack of sexual attraction is normal for asexuals, and lack of romantic feelings is normal for aromantics.

Asexuals, like aromantics, challenge the expectation that everyone wants a romantic, sexual partnership. They don't. Nor do they believe that they would be better off with one.

Single and Alone—or Lonely?

Far from the stereotype of the lonely single, lifelong singles are less lonely than other older people, according to psychologist Bella DePaulo, the author of *Singled Out*. Nor are singles alone.

Many singles have close friendships that are just as valuable as romantic partnerships. But assumptions that friendships are less significant than romantic partnerships hide their value.

Understanding the reasons people have for remaining single might help to handle family stresses. If you're single, you could take unwanted questioning as a teachable moment. If you're the friend or family member of someone who tells you they're happily single—believe them.

Periodical and Internet Sources Bibliography

The following articles have been selected to supplement the diverse views presented in this chapter.

BetterLyf, "The Trouble with Modern Marriage." Retrieved January 5, 2021. https://www.betterlyf.com/articles/relationships/the -trouble-with-modern-marriage/

Neel Burton, M.D., "A Feminist Critique of Marriage," *Psychology Today*, March 27, 2020. https://www.psychologytoday.com/us /blog/hide-and-seek/201708/feminist-critique-marriage

Linda Caroll, "Marriage Must End the Patriarchy or Patriarchy Will End Marriage," Medium, January 8, 2019. https://medium.com /linda-caroll/marriage-must-end-the-patriarchy-or-patriarchy -will-end-the-marriage-6ffecb73151a

D'Vera Cohn, "Census Bureau Proposes Dropping Some Marriage and Divorce Questions," Pew Research Center, December 17, 2014. https://www.pewresearch.org/fact-tank/2014/12/17 /census-bureau-proposes-dropping-some-marriage-and-divorce -questions/

D'Vera Cohn, "How Many Same-Sex Married Couples in the US? Maybe 170,000," Pew Research Center, June 24, 2015. https:// www.pewresearch.org/fact-tank/2015/06/24/how-many-same -sex-married-couples-in-the-u-s-maybe-170000/

Richard Fry, "New Census Data Show More Americans Are Tying the Knot, But Mostly It's the College-Educated," Pew Research Center, February 6, 2014. https://www.pewresearch.org/fact -tank/2014/02/06/new-census-data-show-more-americans-are -tying-the-knot-but-mostly-its-the-college-educated/

Health Talk, "Women's Experiences of Domestic Violence and Abuse." Retrieved January 5, 2021. https://healthtalk.org /womens-experiences-domestic-violence-and-abuse/overview

Nolo, "Issues Affecting Same-sex Couples FAQ." Retrieved January 5, 2021. https://www.nolo.com/legal-encyclopedia/issues-affecting -same-sex-couples-faq.html

Rachael Pace, "20 Most Common Marriage Problems Faced by Married Couples," Marriage.com, August 11, 2020. https://www

.marriage.com/advice/relationship/8-common-problems-in
-married-life/

Danielle Page, "5 Ways Marriage Is Harder in 2017 (And What You Can Do About It)," NBC News, June 6, 2017. https://www
.nbcnews.com/better/relationships/5-ways-marriage-harder
-2017-n768876

Darby Strickland, "Sexual Abuse in Marriage," Christian Counseling & Educational Foundation, June 6, 2018. https://www.ccef.org
/sexual-abuse-in-marriage/

Vox, "We Need to Talk About Sexual Assault in Marriage," March 8, 2018. https://www.vox.com/first-person/2018/3/8/17087628
/sexual-assault-marriage-metoo

Dave Willis, "8 Reasons Modern Marriage Isn't Working," Patheos, January 25, 2016. https://www.patheos.com/blogs/davewillis/8
-reasons-modern-marriage-isnt-working/

CHAPTER 4

What Is the Future of the Institution of Marriage?

Chapter Preface

According to a recent poll, approximately 40 percent of Americans believe that marriage is an obsolete institution, viewing it as perhaps not necessary to live a fulfilling life. And indeed, fewer couples than ever before are getting—and staying— married. At this rate, theorists predict marriage rates will continue to decline in the near future.

The very definition of what constitutes a marriage has changed drastically in the last decade or so. That includes the structural, legal, emotional, and sexual aspects of marriage partnerships. For one, the traditional and legal definition of marriage is no longer defined as only an arrangement between a man and a woman, although some conservative groups are still challenging this. Same-sex marriage is now legal in all 50 states, which means it is now legal for two people of any diverse gender identification to legally wed and enjoy the social, financial, and legal benefits marriage bestows upon partners.

Another clear and drastic change from the conception of marriage of years ago is that when people marry, they no longer assume the marriage will last a lifetime. Divorce is prevalent, with exactly half of all marriages ending in a divorce. Some couples, wanting to offer their former partners dignity and respect, are even creating rituals to acknowledge the end of their unions, calling this "decoupling."

There is much speculation about what marriage will look like in the future, or if the institution will survive at all in the same form we are now familiar with. One basic human need, however, is the propensity of people to look for a primary partner. Read on for diverse viewpoints that prognosticate on the future of marriage.

> *"The marriage promotion industry has spent decades trying to persuade us that the ills of the nation, and perhaps the world, can be blamed on the decline of marriage, and that a reversal of that trend will be the solution."*

The Decline in Marriage Is Part of a Larger Transition Toward Gender Equality

Bella DePaulo

In the following viewpoint, Bella DePaulo argues that efforts by conservative groups to promote marriage in order to "fix" societal problems are misguided. The author uses sociology professor Phillip N. Cohen's book on marriage and inequality, Enduring Bonds, *as her framework, including a look at the initiatives used to promote marriage among poor people and people of color. She suggests that better education, jobs, and income equality would be better ideas for improving society. Bella DePaulo is a social psychologist and the author of numerous books on being single, including* Singled Out: How Singles Are Stereotyped, Stigmatized, and Ignored *and* Still Live Happily Ever After.

"Less Marriage, More Equality?" by Bella DePaulo, Unmarried Equality, March 19, 2018. Reprinted by permission.

As you read, consider the following questions:

1. According to the viewpoint, what is a better indicator of child poverty than a child's parents' marital status?
2. What are the benefits to delaying marriage?
3. How does marriage promote inequality, according to the author?

M arriage is the foundation of a successful society." So proclaimed the 1996 welfare reform act. Since then, more than a billion dollars has been spent to promote marriage (just the "one man, one woman" variety) among the poor.

Conservative think tanks and organizations such as the Heritage Foundation, the Hoover Institution, the Institute for American Values, the Bradley Foundation, and the Templeton Foundation have poured copious resources into the goal of persuading more people to get married. They've funded meetings, symposia, reports, writings for the popular media, ideologically-inspired research, and programs to educate poor people about marriage.

More Marriage and More Marriage Promotion or More Education and More Jobs?

In several chapters of his new book, *Enduring Bonds: Inequality, Marriage, Parenting, and Everything Else that Makes Families Great and Terrible,* University of Maryland Professor of Sociology Philip N. Cohen tells the disturbing story of the rise of the marriage promotion movement. Marriage promotion, Cohen explains, "is mostly about convincing (educating, coaching, coercing) poor people to marry other poor people." The assumption is that "if poor people changed their attitudes (norms, culture) about marriage—if they put more priority on the importance of marriage and worried less about the economic qualities of the match—there would be more marriage. And, marriage promoters say, this would reduce poverty, inequality, violence, and abuse."

Cohen takes on those claims in *Enduring Bonds*. For example, in one set of analyses, he looks at various factors linked to child poverty, starting with marriage. The children of married parents are in fact less likely to be poor than the children who do not have married parents: 9% compared to 15%. But then Cohen presents similar analyses of parents' education and employment. Those factors turn out to be more consequential than marriage. Children living with a college graduate parent are less likely to be poor than those not living with a college graduate parent, 5% compared to 17%. The results are most dramatic for employment. Children living with a parent with full-time year-round employment are far less likely to be poor than those living with a parent who does not have that employment, 7% compared to 40%.

In the marriage education and promotion programs such as the Healthy Marriage Initiative and the Responsible Fatherhood Initiative, couples sometimes spend hours in various training sessions, such as those designed to teach them communication skills. The programs have been evaluated systematically and the results are clear. The billion dollars spent on these efforts—money taken from the federal welfare program—have "unequivocally showed total failure."

An example is a program that was tested in eight locations. Fifteen months afterwards, the couples who participated were no more likely to be married or still together than the couples in the control group.

Marriage Is Headed in One Direction Only: Down

In the big picture, in the US and around the world, marriage trends have been headed in the exact opposite direction that the marriage promoters have been aiming for. For example, between 1950 and 2010, rates of marriage in the US have declined precipitously. In the four decades after 1970, there was "an unprecedented drop of more than 50 percent."

In many nations all around the world, the same declining rate of marriage since the 1970s has been occurring. Even in countries in which nearly everyone eventually marries, people are spending more years of their life single because the age at which they first marry is increasing. As Cohen notes about the slipping rates of marriage, "there are as yet no cases of major developed countries reversing this trend."

A Different Take on Marriage and Inequality

The marriage promotion industry has spent decades trying to persuade us that the ills of the nation, and perhaps the world, can be blamed on the decline of marriage, and that a reversal of that trend will be the solution. Cohen, though, draws from data from 125 nations to document something very different. He looked at the relationship between the proportion of time that people spend married and the degree of gender equality in each country (using a composite measure from the UN). He found that less time spent married is linked to greater gender equality.

"The decline in marriage—people spending a smaller portion of their lives married, on average—is part of a larger global transition toward gender equality." Marriage, Cohen notes, "is most universal in poorer societies, and also those with less gender equality."

Links between society-level trends, such as average time spent married and gender equality, are just suggestive. Methodologically, they don't tell us about causality the way a true experiment would. Different ways of explaining the results can usually be generated. To Cohen, differences in women's education and their participation in the workforce are especially important.

As an example, Cohen compares China and India. Marriage is nearly universal in both nations; about 98 percent of women are married by their early thirties. In India, though, the average age at which women first marry is about 20, whereas in China, it is about 24. In those four extra years that Chinese women stay single, they invest more in their education, they spent more time in the labor force, and they are less likely to have children than their Indian counterparts. China ranks 40th in the world in gender equality; India ranks 130th. "Early, universal marriage," Cohen suggests, "is a key barrier to gender equality."

Solutions: Persuade Single People to Marry or Create a More Equitable Society for Everyone, Regardless of Marital Status?

To the movers and shakers in the marriage promotion movement, societal problems such as growing economic inequality are the fault of single mothers. They are the ones raising boys who will become criminals and girls who will get pregnant while they are still teens and, of course, unmarried. (For some debunking of those kinds of claims, see the brief book *Single Parents and Their Children: The Good News No One Ever Tells You*, as well as the relevant sections of *Enduring Bonds*.)

Cohen, of course, has a whole different view:

> Single mothers are the visible expression of the historical trend toward both gender equality and more diverse family structures, which have had the effect of decentering the married, man-woman, breadwinner-homemaker nuclear family.

Attempts to get more people to marry have not worked, and Cohen does not believe they ever will. Considering "the apparent impossibility of trying to redirect the ship of marriage," he argues, "we have to do what we already know we have to do: *reduce the disadvantages accruing to those who aren't married, or whose parents aren't married.*" [Emphasis is mine.]

Just imagine if someone in Congress seriously proposed one of Cohen's approaches to reducing the disadvantages of the unmarried:

> One obvious solution is to take money away from married high-income people and give it to single low-income people. With all the benefits married people get—many of them through no special efforts of their own, but rather as a result of their social status at birth, race, health, good looks, legal perks, or lucky breaks—it seems reasonable to tax marriage...

Cohen knows how unlikely that is, and suggests an alternative, which is slightly less provocative: "taxing wealth a little more."

A single person can dream.

> *"Married people live longer and healthier lives ... nine out of ten married guys who are alive at 48 will make it to age 65, compared with just six in ten comparable single guys."*

The Institution of Marriage Promotes Health and Well-Being

Maggie Gallagher

In the following viewpoint, Maggie Gallagher uses statistical data to argue the benefits of marriage beyond the protection of children. According to the author, research shows that married people enjoy increased happiness, longevity, satisfaction, economic well-being, and safety. In addition, marriage can bring purpose and meaning to one's life. Maggie Gallagher is a writer, socially conservative commenter, and activist. She is a cofounder of the National Organization for Marriage.

As you read, consider the following questions:

1. What reasons does the author list that marriage is good for people in general?
2. Are these benefits basically the same for both sexes?
3. Beyond economic benefits, what are some of the benefits of staying married, according to the viewpoint?

"Why Marriage Is Good for You," by Maggie Gallagher, Manhattan Institute for Policy Research, Inc., Autumn 2000. Reprinted by permission.

When Americans debate the value of marriage, most attention focuses on the potential harm to children of divorce or illegitimacy, and for good reason. Mountains of research tell us that children reared outside of intact marriages are much more likely than other kids to slip into poverty, become victims of child abuse, fail at school and drop out, use illegal drugs, launch into premature sexual activity, become unwed teen mothers, divorce, commit suicide and experience other signs of mental illness, become physically ill, and commit crimes and go to jail. On average, children reared outside of marriage are less successful in their careers, even after controlling not only for income but also for parental conflict.

Yes, marriage protects children. And yes, marriage therefore protects taxpayers and society from a broad and deep set of costs, personal and communal. But there is another case for marriage, equally significant, that you probably haven't heard. Marriage is a powerful creator and sustainer of human and social capital for adults as well as children, about as important as education when it comes to promoting the health, wealth, and well-being of adults and communities. For most Americans, this is news. When it comes to adults, the case for lifelong marriage has been framed in exclusively moral, spiritual, and emotional terms: one side argues for personal liberation from marriage, the other urges parents to sacrifice for God's and/or the kids' sake.

These are important considerations to be sure. Parents surely should be willing to make appropriate sacrifices for their kids' sake. But framing the marriage debate solely in those terms obscures as much as it reveals. It misses the profound benefits that lasting marriage confers on adults. And it overestimates considerably the likelihood that divorce will, in fact, lead to greater happiness for the individual.

Recently, I had the opportunity to review the scientific evidence on the consequences of marriage for adults with University of Chicago scholar Linda J. Waite for our new book, *The Case for Marriage*. What I found surprised me. Quietly, with little fanfare, a broad and deep body of scientific literature has been accumulating that affirms what Genesis teaches: it is not good for man to be alone—no, nor woman neither. In virtually every way that social scientists can measure, married people do much better than the unmarried or divorced: they live longer, healthier, happier, sexier, and more affluent lives.

How big a difference does marriage make? If David Letterman were to compile a Top Ten list for marriage, it might look something like this:

Top Ten Reasons Why Marriage Is Good for You

10. It's Safer

Marriage lowers the risk that both men and women will become victims of violence, including domestic violence. A 1994 Justice Department report, based on the National Crime Victimization Survey, found that single and divorced women were four to five times more likely to be victims of violence in any given year than wives; bachelors were four times more likely to be violent-crime victims than husbands. Two-thirds of acts of violence against women committed by intimate partners were not committed by husbands but by boyfriends (whether live-in or not) or former husbands or boyfriends. As one scholar sums up the relevant research: "Regardless of methodology, the studies yielded similar results: cohabitors engage in more violence than spouses." Linda Waite conducted an analysis of the National Survey of Families and Households for our new book. She found that, even after controlling for education, race, age, and gender, people who live together are still three times more likely to say their arguments got physical (such as kicking, hitting, or shoving) in the past year than married couples.

9. It Can Save Your Life

Married people live longer and healthier lives. The power of marriage is particularly evident in late middle age. When Linda Waite and a colleague, for example, analyzed mortality differentials in a very large, nationally representative sample, they found an astonishingly large "marriage gap" in longevity: nine out of ten married guys who are alive at 48 will make it to age 65, compared with just six in ten comparable single guys (controlling for race, education, and income). For women, the protective benefits of marriage are also powerful, though not quite as large. Nine out of ten wives alive at age 48 will live to be senior citizens, compared with just eight out of ten divorced and single women.

In fact, according to statisticians Bernard Cohen and I-Sing Lee, who compiled a catalog of relative mortality risks, "being unmarried is one of the greatest risks that people voluntarily subject themselves to." Having heart disease, for example, reduces a man's life expectancy by just under six years, while being unmarried chops almost ten years off a man's life. This is not just a selection effect: even controlling for initial health status, sick people who are married live longer than their unmarried counterparts. Having a spouse, for example, lowers a cancer patient's risk of dying from the disease as much as being in an age category ten years younger. A recent study of outcomes for surgical patients found that just being married lowered a patient's risk of dying in the hospital. For perhaps more obvious reasons, the risk a hospital patient will be discharged to a nursing home was two and a half times greater if the patient was unmarried. Scientists who have studied immune functioning in the laboratory find that happily married couples have better-functioning immune systems. Divorced people, even years after the divorce, show much lower levels of immune function.

8. It Can Save Your Kid's Life

Children lead healthier, longer lives if parents get and stay married. Adults who fret about second-hand smoke and drunk driving would do well to focus at least some of their attention on this point. In one long-term study that followed a sample of highly advantaged children (middle-class whites with IQs of at least 135) up through their seventies, a parent's divorce knocked four years off the adult child's life expectancy. Forty-year-olds from divorced homes were three times more likely to die from all causes than 40-year-olds whose parents stayed married.

7. You Will Earn More Money

Men today tend to think of marriage as a consumption item—a financial burden. But a broad and deep body of scientific literature suggests that for men especially, marriage is a productive institution—as important as education in boosting a man's earnings. In fact, getting a wife may increase an American male's salary by about as much as a college education. Married men make, by some estimates, as much as 40 percent more money than comparable single guys, even after controlling for education and job history. The longer a man stays married, the higher the marriage premium he receives. Wives' earnings also benefit from marriage, but they decline when motherhood enters the picture. Childless white wives get a marriage wage premium of 4 percent, and black wives earn 10 percent more than comparable single women.

6. Did I Mention You'll Get Much Richer?

Married people not only make more money, they manage money better and build more wealth together than either would alone. At identical income levels, for example, married people are less likely to report "economic hardship" or trouble paying basic bills. The longer you stay married, the more assets you build; by contrast, length of cohabitation has no relationship to wealth accumulation. On the verge of retirement, the average married couple has accumulated assets worth about $410,000, compared with $167,000 for the never-married and $154,000 for the divorced. Couples who stayed married in one study saw their assets increase twice as fast as those who had remained divorced over a five-year period.

5. You'll Tame His Cheatin' Heart (Hers, Too)

Marriage increases sexual fidelity. Cohabiting men are four times more likely to cheat than husbands, and cohabiting women are eight times more likely to cheat than wives. Marriage is also the only realistic promise of permanence in a romantic relationship.

Just one out of ten cohabiting couples are still cohabiting after five years. By contrast, 80 percent of couples marrying for the first time are still married five years later, and close to 60 percent (if current divorce rates continue) will marry for life. One British study found that biological parents who marry are three times more likely still to be together two years later than biological two-parent families who cohabit, even after controlling for maternal age, education, economic hardship, previous relationship failure, depression, and relationship quality. Marriage may be riskier than it once was, but when it comes to making love last, there is still no better bet.

4. You Won't Go Bonkers

Marriage is good for your mental health. Married men and women are less depressed, less anxious, and less psychologically distressed than single, divorced, or widowed Americans. By contrast, getting divorced lowers both men's and women's mental health, increasing depression and hostility, and lowering one's self-esteem and sense of personal mastery and purpose in life.

And this is not just a statistical illusion: careful researchers who have tracked individuals as they move toward marriage find that it is not just that happy, healthy people marry; instead, getting married gives individuals a powerful mental health boost. Nadine Marks and James Lambert looked at changes in the psychological health of a large sample of Americans in the late eighties and early nineties. They measured psychological well-being at the outset and then watched what happened to individuals over the next years as they married, remained single, or divorced. When people married, their mental health improved—consistently and substantially. When people divorced, they suffered substantial deterioration in mental and emotional well-being, including increases in depression and declines in reported happiness. Those who divorced over this period also reported a lower sense of personal mastery, less positive relations with others, less sense of purpose in life, and lower levels of self-acceptance than their married peers did.

Married men are only half as likely as bachelors and one-third as likely as divorced guys to take their own lives. Wives are also much less likely to commit suicide than single, divorced, or widowed women. Married people are much less likely to have problems with alcohol abuse or illegal drugs. In a recent national survey, one out of four single men ages 19 to 26 say their drinking causes them problems at work or problems with aggression, compared with just one out of seven married guys this age.

3. It Will Make You Happy

For most people, the joys of the single life and of divorce are overrated. Overall, 40 percent of married people, compared with about a quarter of singles or cohabitors, say they are "very happy" with life in general. Married people are also only about half as likely as singles or cohabitors to say they are unhappy with their lives.

How happy are the divorced? If people divorce in order to be happy, as we are often told, the majority should demand their money back. Just 18 percent of divorced adults say they are "very happy," and divorced adults are twice as likely as married folk to say they are "not too happy" with life in general. Only a minority of divorcing adults go on to make marriages that are happier than the one they left. "Divorce or be miserable," certain cultural voices tell us, but, truth be told, "Divorce and be miserable" is at least as likely an outcome.

This is not just an American phenomenon. One recent study by Steven Stack and J. Ross Eshleman of 17 developed nations found that "married persons have a significantly higher level of happiness than persons who are not married," even after controlling for gender, age, education, children, church attendance, financial satisfaction, and self-reported health. Further, "the strength of the association between being married and being happy is remarkably consistent across nations." Marriage boosted financial satisfaction and health. But being married conferred a happiness advantage over and above its power to improve the pocketbook and the health chart. Cohabitation, by contrast, did not increase financial satisfaction or perceived health, and the boost to happiness from having a live-in lover was only about a quarter of that of being married. Another large study, of 100,000 Norwegians, found that, with both men and women, "the married have the highest level of subjective well-being, followed by the widowed." Even long-divorced people who cohabited were not any happier than singles.

2. Your Kids Will Love You More
Divorce weakens the bonds between parents and children over the long run. Adult children of divorce describe relationships with both their mother and their father less positively, on average, and they are about 40 percent less likely than adults from intact marriages to say they see either parent at least several times a week.

1. You'll Have Better Sex, More Often
Despite the lurid *Sex in the City* marketing that promises singles erotic joys untold, both husbands and wives are more likely to report that they have an extremely satisfying sex life than are singles or cohabitors. (Divorced women were the least likely to have a sex life they found extremely satisfying emotionally.) For one thing, married people are more likely to have a sex life. Single men are 20 times more likely, and single women ten times more likely, not to have had sex even once in the past year than the married. (Almost a quarter of single guys and 30 percent of single women lead sexless lives.)

Married people are also the most likely to report a highly satisfying sex life. Wives, for example, are almost twice as likely as divorced and never-married women to have a sex life that a) exists and b) is extremely satisfying emotionally. Contrary to popular lore, for men, having a wife beats shacking up by a wide margin: 50 percent of husbands say sex with their partner is extremely satisfying physically, compared with 39 percent of cohabiting men.

The Power of the Social Institution

How can a piece of paper work such miracles? For surprisingly, the piece of paper, and not just the personal relationship, matters a great deal. People who live together, for the most part, don't reap the same kinds of benefits that men and women who marry do. Something about marriage as a social institution—a shared aspiration and a public, legal vow—gives wedlock the power to change individuals' lives.

By increasing confidence that this partnership will last, marriage allows men and women to specialize—to take on those parts of life's tasks, from developing an interesting social life to getting money out of insurance companies, that one person does better or enjoys more than the other. Though this specialization is often along traditional gender lines, it doesn't have to be. Even childless married couples benefit from splitting up the work. Married households have twice the talent, twice the time, and twice the labor pool of singles. Over time, as spouses specialize, each actually produces more in both market and non-market goods than singles who have to shoulder all of life's tasks on their own.

But because marriage is a partnership in the whole of life, backed up by family, community, and religious values, marriage can do what economic partnerships don't: give a greater sense of meaning and purpose to life (a reason to exercise or cut back on booze, work harder, and to keep plugging even in the middle of those times when the marriage may not feel gratifying at all). Married people are both responsible for and responsible to another human being, and both halves of that dynamic lead the married to live more responsible, fruitful, and satisfying lives. Marriage is a transformative act, changing the way two people look at each other, at the future, and at their roles in society. And it changes the way significant others—from family to congregation to insurance companies and the IRS—look at and treat that same couple. Sexual fidelity, an economic union, a parenting alliance, the promise of care that transcends day-to-day emotions: all these are what give a few words mumbled before a clergyman or judge the power to change lives.

What proportion of unhappily married couples who stick it out stay miserable? The latest data show that within five years, just 12 percent of very unhappily married couples who stick it out are still unhappy; 70 percent of the unhappiest couples now describe their marriage as "very" or "quite" happy.

Just as good marriages go bad, bad marriages go good. And they have a better chance of doing so in a society that recognizes the value of marriage than one that sings the statistically dubious joys of divorce.

> *"People see that nearly half of all marriages end in divorce and so they are less willing to take the risk and get married."*

In the United Kingdom, Marriage Is on the Decline

ReviseSociology

In the following viewpoint, authors from ReviseSociology argue that the institution of marriage has been on a sharp decline for decades in England and Wales. The decline of marriage is not as simple as individual choice; there are general social changes behind its decline. Reasons include changing gender roles, regard for individual rights and freedoms before marriage, and a risk aversion to getting a divorce. ReviseSociology is an educational website based in the United Kingdom.

As you read, consider the following questions:

1. Is declining marriage specific only to Wales and England?
2. According to the viewpoint, what reasons are behind the overall decline in marriage?
3. How does individuality affect the rate of marriage, according to the authors?

"Explaining the Changing Patterns of Marriage," ReviseSociology.com, February 7, 2017. Reprinted by permission.

There has been a long term decline in the number of marriages in England and Wales.

In the late 1960s and early 1970s there were over 400,000 marriages a year, by 2017 there were just under 250,000 marriages a year.

Although the decline seems to have slowed recently, and even increased since 2008. Other trends include:

- People are more likely to cohabit (although in most cases this is a step before marriage)
- People are marrying later
- The number of remarriages has increased
- Couples are less likely to marry in church
- There is a greater diversity of marriages (greater ethnic diversity and civil partnerships)
- There has been a very recent increase in the marriage rate
- Most households are still headed by a married couple
- Couples may cohabit, but this is normally before getting married—they just get married later
- Most people still think marriage is the ideal type of relationship
- The fact that remarriages have increased show that people still value the institution of marriage

Economic Factors—The Increasing Cost of Living and the Increasing Cost of Weddings

Increasing property prices in recent years may be one of the factors why couples choose to get married later in life. The average deposit on a first time home is now over £30,000, with the average cost of a wedding being around £18,000. So for most couples it is literally a choice between getting married in their 20s and then renting/living with parents, or buying a house first and then getting married in their 30s. The second option is obviously the more financially rational.

Open Marriages

Couples may still not be comfortable to talk about their open marriages, but experts say the more we make them less of a secret, the less "dirty" the concept becomes.

"They need to be normalized just like monogamy has been," Ottawa-based matchmaker with Friend of a Friend Matchmaking, Ceilidhe Wynn, tells Global News. "When monogamous people start to realize that open marriages and polyamorous relationships are often just the same as monogamous ones—just with more people—acceptance can happen."

And while there are no hard statistics on how many couples are in open marriages in Canada, experts say it can range from both young people in their 20s, as well as people in their 40s. The older crowd often feels like they've missed out on exploring themselves sexually when they were younger, says relationship expert and couples' therapist Nicole McCance.

But there's a reason there are still negative connotations attached to this option of marriage, and typically, it has to do with monogamy.

"We're told that monogamy is the 'right' way to do relationships and anything outside of that is seen as 'cheating.' But relationships and love aren't so black and white," Wynn explains.

Changing Gender Roles

Liberal Feminists point to changing gender roles as one of the main reasons why couples get married later. More than half of the workforce is now female, which means that most women do not have to get married in order to be financially secure. In fact, according to the theory of the genderquake, the opposite is happening—now that most jobs are in the service sector, economic power is shifting to women, meaning that marriage seems like a poor option for women in a female economy.

Dr. Tammy Nelson, a sex and relationship expert and author of *The New Monogamy*, says an open marriage was once defined as swinging, especially in the '70s, and in popular movies like *Bob & Carol & Ted & Alice* and the book *Open Marriages* by George and Nena O'Neill.

"For some couples, an open marriage means that you have a committed, intimate relationship with your partner, but sometimes you share a sexual experience, like going to sex clubs or on swingers vacations," she tells Global News. "Each partner will have implicit assumptions about what opening a marriage might mean."

Nelson says in order for an open marriage to work, both parties need to have a discussion on the monogamy agreement, including establishing the rules, negotiations, and what counts as "open."

"Everything should be a 'talk-about-able' thing," she says. "Sometimes your vision of an open relationship might be different than your partner's. The real takeaway regarding open marriage is that it means you need open communication."

But it also can have downfalls

McCance says in her line of work with clients, typically, most people hold onto the idea of a traditional marriage and monogamy.

"Open Marriages Are a Lot More Functional Than You Think," by Arti Patel, Global News, June 11, 2017.

The New Right

Blame the decline of marriage on moral decline—part of the broader breakdown of social institutions and due to too much acceptance of diversity. This results in the inability of people to commit to each other, and they see this as bad for society and the socialisation of the next generation.

Postmodernisation

Postmodernists explain the decline in marriage as a result of the move to postmodern consumer society characterised by greater individual choice and freedom. We are used to being consumers and picking and choosing, and so marriage is now a matter of individual choice.

Another process associated with postmodernisation is the decline of tradition and religion (secularisation)—as a result there is less social stigma attached to cohabiting or remarrying after a divorce.

Late Modernism

Associated with the ideas of Anthony Giddens and Ulrich Beck— argues that the decline in marriage is not as simple as people simply having more freedom—people are less likely to get married because of structural changes making life more uncertain. People may want to get married, but living in a late-modern world means marriage doesn't seem like a sensible option.

Ulrich Beck argues that fewer people getting married is because of an increase in "risk consciousness"—people see that nearly half of all marriages end in divorce and so they are less willing to take the risk and get married.

Beck also talks about individualisation—a new social norm is that our individual desires are more important than social commitments, and this makes marriage less likely.

Giddens builds on this and says that the typical relationship today is the Pure Relationship—one which lasts only as long as both partners are happy with it, not because of tradition or a sense of commitment. This makes cohabitation and serial monogamy rather than the long term commitment of a marriage more likely.

> *"Women, having gained power economically and politically, now have a real say in our fate. And for many of us, marriage remains an embodiment of powerlessness."*

Marriage Is in a Delay, Not in a Decline

Rose Hackman

In the following viewpoint, Rose Hackman argues that it is not true that changing sexual norms are to blame for a decline in marriages. The claim that easier access to sex has turned people off of long-term commitments is insulting to both women and men, the author writes. There are a host of more complicated reasons for changing attitudes toward marriage, including advances in women's rights, the economy, and desire for strong partnerships. Rose Hackman is a British journalist based in Detroit. She was a features writer for the Guardian.

As you read, consider the following questions:

1. According to the viewpoint, is marriage in the United States actually in decline?
2. How do economic differences affect marriage success rates?
3. Why do many women equate marriage with powerlessness, according to the author?

"Is Marriage Really on the Decline Because of Men's Cheap Access to Sex?" Rose Hackman, Guardian News and Media Limited, June 11, 2018. Reprinted by permission.

L ast week, I read an article published in the *Wall Street Journal* claiming that marriage was on the decline because of men's cheap access to sex.

The argument of the article, by sociologist Mark Regnerus, didn't go much further than the age-old adage: nobody will buy the cow if you're giving away the milk for free. Regnerus is affiliated with a conservative, Christian thinktank in Texas that local news once dubbed the "no-sex" institute.

"Many women today expect little in return for sex, in terms of time, attention, commitment or fidelity," Regnerus claims. "Men, in turn, do not feel compelled to supply these goods as they once did. It is the new sexual norm for Americans."

Women, Regnerus continues, "are hoping to find good men without supporting the sexual norms that would actually make men better."

More astonishing than seeing this theory published in the *Wall Street Journal* was seeing the degree of viral popularity the article still enjoyed nine months after it was first published. Do people really believe women are responsible for the decline of marriage because we are having sex too much, and men no longer have any incentive to pair up?

I found the argument dehumanizing to both genders, and decided to explore its veracity.

I made calls to experts on both sides of the Atlantic. My favorite conversation, though, was with an unmarried male friend who loves pursuing women, and who has so far resisted the siren call of marriage. We'll call him Tim.

"Tim, are you not married because women are providing sex too easily?" I ask.

Tim, who never appears to have a lull in enthusiastic female dating partners—all on a steady, respectful roster— answers carefully.

"No, I don't agree with that. If I were to agree with that, it would also imply that people only get married to have sex. Yes, they overlap, but you don't do one to do the other."

I knew he would give me thoughtful answers.

"I see marriage as a partnership, almost like a business. You want the company to grow and be as big as you want it to be: being able to have kids, to go to this country … The process of that building, that's what I see marriage being about."

Tim is a few years shy of 40. He says the fact that he hasn't married yet doesn't mean he won't in the future. For him, however, him being the right kind of partner is just as important as finding the right person to partner with.

The Money Factor

"Marriage is not in decline, it is in delay," says historian Stephanie Coontz, author of *Marriage, a History* and director of research and public education at the Council on Contemporary Families.

She points out that the percentage of Americans expected to marry by early middle age—around 80%—is remarkably similar to what it was 50 years ago.

Yet Regnerus claims marriage in the US is in "open retreat." Focusing on Americans between the ages of 25 and 34, he states that 55% of this age group was married in 2000 but only 40% in 2015.

Coontz explains what I already know to be anecdotally true, having graduated college in 2008, the year the economy collapsed: both women and men want to be economically and educationally set before they marry—an ambition increasingly harder for a generational cohort facing crippling debt, poor healthcare and an economy where stable career ladders have been replaced by part-time freelance gigs.

Watching half of our parents' generation get divorced was probably not the biggest advertisement for marriage either. But dragging our feet may end up helping us on that front too. If you care about the quality of the marriage you enter into, putting marriage off is good thinking: marrying young heightens the probability of divorce, and the longer people know each other before tying the knot the more likely they are to stay together.

The one group where marriage appears to be in actual decline, rather than delay, is adults who are at the very bottom of the socio-economic hierarchy.

For the working poor, getting married is hardly a guarantee of ascendance, explains Amy Traub, an associate director of policy and research at the thinktank Demos. She highlights the reality of surviving with low wages, no paid sick leave, no paid parental leave, and no subsidized childcare. Traub's research shows that a married couple will see their income go down by 14% after they have a child.

Coontz adds that studies on groups struggling economically reveal that women, not men, are the ones deferring marriage for the sake of financial stability.

At the opposite end of the spectrum, the group most likely to get married? Highly educated women, who are using their economic independence to renegotiate when and how they enter into an institution that previously required their gender subservience.

The Sex Factor

Regnerus's argument—which relegates men to brainless automatons whose only on-button for productivity and planning is sex—does little to reinvent or challenge oppressive gender stereotypes.

It also overlooks the fact that millennials, despite dating apps and the moral panic around hookup culture, actually have sex with fewer partners than their elders, not more. Our average number of sexual partners is eight—markedly lower than Gen X (10 partners) or baby boomers (11).

My friend Tim explains that while seduction and the prospect of sex can motivate him into action, it is insulting to think it is the be-all and end-all of male behavior.

Tim also has a hard time grappling with Regnerus's logic, which has women convincing men to commit using the one tool he allows us: the ability to grant or withhold sexual intercourse.

"Eventually, if you got the cow just for the milk, that milk loses its appeal," Tim says, challenging part of Regnerus's premise. "That's not enough," Tim exclaims. "The milk is not enough!"

If the framing is insufficient for Tim, now may also be a good moment to point out that women not only seek out sex, but also have growing expectations about quality and pleasure. A male-centric and reductive view of sexuality is painfully outdated.

Caroline Rusterholz, a historian of sexuality at Birkbeck College, University of London, says that the idea of harmonious sex within marriage began in the 1930s—enabled by the publication of pamphlets and the first opening of family clinics, among other factors—but ideas about sex were taught in ways in line with gender expectations of the time.

"The wife is a musical instrument that the husband plays. The husband is the art maker. The wife is the recipient," says Rusterholz of understandings dating back 80 years.

People believed female orgasms were properly attained through vaginal penetration only, and that the clitoris served only to awaken desire on the path to penetration. This despite studies showing that women mainly attain orgasms by clitoral stimulation, Rusterholz says.

Women started claiming a right to their own bodies and their own sexuality during the feminist liberation movement of the 1970s. But stereotypes and falsehoods about sex didn't always change accordingly.

Society still expects women to be less sexually active, says Rusterholz. "We expect them to be turned towards maintaining relationships. And only having sex when they are in love."

But many of us are fed up with double standards. My generation of women have high hopes and loud voices when it comes to challenging the notion of being passive penis recipients—something expressed clearly during the recent #MeToo movement, a continuation of the liberation movement started decades earlier.

The Independence Factor

I spoke to a female friend—let's call her Jay—who is in a long-term heterosexual relationship. She wants to establish herself professionally before she considers taking the leap to marriage, even if she has a partner she wants to marry.

When I ask why marriage appeals to her, her language is focused around partnership, egalitarianism, common goals and mutual care.

"I don't think people realize the extent to which, in the 1950s, marriage was non-voluntary," says Philip Cohen, a professor of sociology at the University of Maryland and the author of *Enduring Bonds*, a book on marriage and inequality.

In the mid-20th century, marriage was close to socially mandatory for both genders: women had few economic survival avenues outside marriage and, paradoxically, unmarried men faced job discrimination. That the institution has become more voluntary is a thing to be celebrated, Cohen says, especially for women.

What is entirely absent from Regnerus's male-centric argument is the fact that women, having gained power economically and politically, now have a real say in our fate. And for many of us, marriage remains an embodiment of powerlessness.

"Married men gained rights over women's bodies, property and children," confirms Clare Chambers, a lecturer in philosophy at the University of Cambridge who wrote a book arguing for an end to state-recognized marriage. "Traditionally [marriage] has maintained legal gender inequality, and it has done so to the benefit of men."

Chambers concedes that many formal inequalities tied to marriage have been denounced and revoked. Marital rape was outlawed in the UK in 1991 and in the US in 1993—hard to believe there was ever an exemption—and same-sex marriage was legalized in 2014 and 2015 respectively.

Last fall I wrote a callout for the *Guardian*, as research for a book on the invisible load of emotional labor many women bear.

One of the women who responded told me: "I married my husband in 1979. He was 24, I was 20. Three times in the first five years of marriage he demanded sex and when I adamantly said no, he basically raped me. That created a negative environment of hatred from me. I ended up dreading sex and being repulsed by men. We stopped having sex when I had early menopause (thank goodness)."

Sexual availability was traditionally understood as a woman's marital obligation. Although no longer legally enforced, that troubling paradigm is only reinforced by claims that women must restrain their premarital sexual activity if they want to attract a husband.

Women may be equal before the law, but these kinds of deep-seated, disturbing beliefs surrounding marriage roles don't exactly entice us to rush into marrying.

The Chores Factor

Sexism within marriage still runs deep—in more ways than one.

Studies consistently show that women perform more unpaid housework than men, and that men are able to devote more time to leisure activities. Stephanie Coontz, the historian, quotes a study which found that getting married adds seven hours a week to a woman's unpaid labor workload—while decreasing a man's by one hour.

And that's not even counting the exhausting and chronic performance of emotional labor, a term describing the invisible work—at home as well as on the job—that women put into being thoughtful, forward-thinking and caring; managing others' feelings and tempers; and cultivating a functional and happy environment. Since these traits are seen as female, their execution often falls on women's shoulders.

Following the same emotional labor callout mentioned earlier, another woman wrote to me. A feminist in her 60s with a PhD, she described a home environment where her husband, at least when it came to chores and tasks, pulled his weight.

But what fell to her, on top of her own chores and full-time job, was emotionally supporting her husband and children, managing their moods, scheduling their activities and always being emotionally available. Slammed doors were her fault, she says, and her burden to fix.

"Because, of course, the maintenance of peace was my job too," she writes.

Emotional labor is one of the last big problems we need to formally fix—but fixing it requires challenging the most rooted of gendered behaviors.

My source, the feminist in her 60s, continues: "Many women live with partners who can be loving, generous and warm one minute and harshly mansplain or lay down the law the next, silencing women with their power. Who have little understanding for the feelings of others because they don't have to—the woman handles that and covers for them both."

Reinventing rules and being less stringent around fixed gender roles could prove a win-win for all. Studies reveal that egalitarian couples—those who, for example, divide chores equally—have a better and more prolific sex life.

"Choreplay," as the *Chicago Tribune* once put it.

One of the Most Resilient Institutions

Women are far from the only factors in change. Evan Wolfson, founder of Freedom to Marry, one of the bipartisan organizations that successfully campaigned for gay marriage in the United States, has clear views on whether we can blame easy sex for marriage declines.

"Anyone who thinks that marriage is just or primarily about sex knows little about marriage and probably little about sex," says Wolfson, who has been married for seven years.

Wolfson was in a relationship with his now-husband for 10 years before they were able to marry by law. "We already had the love, the sex, the commitment. And now we have the affirmation and the tangible and intangible commitment that comes with it, with equal dignity before the law."

For same-sex couples, of course, marriage is going through a boom simply because it is something that was not an option until a few years ago.

Wolfson believes that instead of embracing or rejecting an outmoded understanding of marriage, the solution lies in changing it for the better. "Marriage is one of the absolutely most resilient institutions. Its history is a history of change."

Romance is certainly not dead. Last month, as 29 million Americans watched Prince Harry and Meghan Markle coyly gaze into each other's eyes as they wed, it became apparent how widespread dreams of love and marriage still are.

But their wedding was also the symbol of an evolution, and a partial break from former rules. That marriage has become more voluntary, that we are hoping to shape it to our own ideals of equality, that we are making up our own minds and own timeline to marriage—these are surely changes to be celebrated. If you want to hurry us along, raise wages, share the mental load as well as the washing load, learn more accurate anatomy and read about consent. And if that still doesn't work, well, leave us the hell alone.

> "Why should anyone have to pass a government's arbitrary, and usually archaic, notion of what constitutes a stable relationship to obtain benefits?"

The Reasons People Normally Cite for Getting Hitched No Longer Make Sense

Tauriq Moosa

In the following viewpoint, Tauriq Moosa argues that perhaps marriage is not all that is promised to people when they walk down the aisle. The author suggests economic reasons and legalities as horrible reasons to get married and says that societies should make policies toward equality rather than push marriage as an institution for a solution to problems. Tauriq Moosa is a South African writer who focuses on ethics, justice, technology, and pop culture.

As you read, consider the following questions:

1. Why is marriage not a good deal, according to the author?
2. Why are economic and institutional reasons not a good reason for people to get married, according to this viewpoint?
3. Why are marriage and love two different things, according to the author?

"We Need to Have a Frank Discussion About Marriage," by Tauriq Moosa, Guardian News and Media Limited, January 4, 2014. Reprinted by permission.

Marriage, as most know it in western countries, is regarded as the end goal of a relationship between (usually) a man and woman, and it normally has some sort of religious component. Marriage is regarded as "sacred." Weddings are planned that few really want to attend; pointless dresses are worn never to be seen again; awkward family photos are taken.

Being married supposedly conveys respectability. We regard it as "settling down," indicative of stability. For some reason we even congratulate people who are already in a relationship for, basically, signing papers (or just changing Facebook statuses) and calling it an engagement. We spend unnecessarily large amounts on engagement and wedding rings.

Yet, with low marriage rates (the US marriage rate is the lowest it's been in a century) and high divorce rates, more single (by choice) parents (not to mention gay marriage), increasing numbers of people abandoning religious traditions as a whole, and people living happier lives because they only even consider marriage later, we should thoroughly reassess the importance of marriage.

Indeed, well-known people have already done so: Oprah Winfrey unashamedly remains unmarried to her life partner of 20 years; powerful Hollywood couple Brad Pitt and Angelina have children, adopted and biological, but remain unmarried. Many of those who live in the public eye are unafraid of dismissing marriage as the end goal. They don't need a marriage certificate or label to be happy.

Thus, why get married at all?

Marriage Myth 1: It's Tradition

One response usually involves tradition, religion, family and/or culture. None of these is sufficient, however, for marriage—or any activity.

To act solely according to what families want would be not only archaic but immoral: just because someone wants something doesn't mean he should get it nor that his demand is right. Parents who, for example, force their child into marriage are increasingly being regarded as committing a crime in westernised countries. Their mere desire doesn't make forced marriage right. A parental desire doesn't have automatic moral soundness (let alone legality).

Love shouldn't be completely unconditional, but it also shouldn't be a gun to the throat. It is our lives, and compromises can usually—but not always—be reached.

Getting married for the sake of your religion also seems problematic: aside from those who are not religious, actions aren't right just because a religion demands them.

Marriage Myth 2: It's a Public Declaration of Love

The second argument you often hear is that marriage is a declaration of love. It's about "showing" we're settled, our partners are "off the market," and we're in a position to build a family. Most of this, however, is a display for others. Plenty of monogamous couples maintain stable, healthy relationships without rings or certificates to "prove" loyalty.

Indeed, who are we trying to prove our love to? Our proof should be our treatment of each other: anything else is addition, not basis. There is more to be worried about if we need to "secure" someone, like a raging animal, with a ring or certificate or other public stamp.

Furthermore, as high divorce rates show, being tied to one person doesn't work out for many, especially for the rest of our lives. Compromises can be made. Couples now swing, maintain open marriages, and so on. But this should only make us question why we're still devoted to the "one true love" ideal in the first place.

Marriage Myth 3: Married Couples Make Better Parents

Of course, there's evidence to support the idea that married couples make better parents and families than, say, single parents. Some of this is because there hasn't been much research into alternative family structures, although that will likely change since trends are changing.

All that said, it's not marriage alone that gives couples magical parent powers: it's the stability of a home, a good relationship, a great support basis. Certificates and rings don't do that: mature, honest, good people do—for themselves and each other. And, further, the assumption that every adult or couple wants children is false.

Marriage Myth 4: You Get Better Legal and Financial Benefits

There's no denying this as perhaps the best of the terrible reasons for marriage. Married couples get certain legal and economic benefits we otherwise can't get. The 1,138 benefits in the US alone

THE BEST MOVIES ABOUT MARRIAGE

The best movies for married couples are often movies about married couples and they can show both sides of the coin: Marriage can be hard; spending all of your waking time with the same person, day after day can be exhausting. But at the same time it can be the best, sweetest, decision you'll ever make. Since marriage is for life it makes perfect sense that so many movies would look at the drama (and comedy) and unfolds in so many marriages. In fact, some of the film industry's greatest movies are about marriage, second marriages, or finding romance after marriage.

The movies featured on this list sometimes provide great inspirational messages, like the idea of never giving up on the one you love the most, no matter the cost. Others are comedies, looking at how difficult the first few years of marriage really are, as in the *Just Married*. No matter what kind of genre you're craving (like Christian movies about marriage) there's sure to be a movie on this list that you and your significant other will love.

1. Father of the Bride
2. Just Married
3. The Notebook
4. My Big, Fat Greek Wedding
5. When a Man Loves a Woman

"Movies About Marriage," by filozsofia, November 19, 2013.

are noteworthy, as many are all over the world. Social security, property, visitation rights, travel benefits and tax breaks. It's an express option on tax filing, health and travel (not exactly romantic. *The Book of Common Prayer* should read: "Till taxes do us part.")

Any marriage solely for tax benefits needs help. It doesn't tell us anything about the relationship itself, save that the couple want benefits from the state. It's not that much different from the infamous "green card" scenarios, where citizenship is obtained or a visa extended due to marrying a local. But this, too, undermines what many think marriage is—or should be.

Further, we should question why only one kind of relationship is recognised: namely the monogamous kind. Monogamy should be an option, not mandatory, on any level—let alone the legal and financial.

You could argue that the state needs some way to recognise stability. If marriage is the only way, then perhaps the state and I can nod and wink as we pass each other our papers for our mutual benefit. Similarly, this assumes the state should be involved in marriage at all, which itself requires serious consideration. If as adults we can decide how to spend the rest our lives, we can, on a case-by-case basis, say, draw up legal documents. Then, as Edward Morrisey points out:

> Those who choose to cohabit in non-traditional relationships have ample options for formalizing their arrangements through [this] private contract process, which government enforces but does not sanction. That leaves adults free to choose whatever sexual arrangements they desire outside of the actual prohibitions that are objectively applied to everyone. That is actual freedom and equality.

Thus, if possible, even for these important economic and legal reasons marriage appears unnecessary. In the UK, for example, people can draw up similar documents to those of married couples. There's no reason unmarried but cohabiting couples should be denied those rights earmarked solely for the married.

Why should anyone have to pass a government's arbitrary, and usually archaic, notion of what constitutes a stable relationship to obtain benefits? If much can be done from a legal and contractual side without marriage, then marriage loses all credibility.

The "sanctity" of marriage—whatever that really means—has long been undermined for conservatives by: high divorce rates, polyandry and polygamy, gay marriage, recognition that there's no "one" way marriage has always been, and so on. But, aside from these, we should wonder at marriage's necessity.

We want a society in which we're all treated equally like adults. Marriage as the assumed end goal of social life creates a stigma on unmarried people who are viewed as, for example, less stable, meaning they're less likely to be able to adopt children—despite such people being as stable as married people.

My point isn't eradication of marriage, but rethinking marriage's importance and assumptions. This could help open all people up to different kinds of sexual and romantic interactions they might otherwise never experience—or, at the very least, increase tolerance, since society isn't rewarding only one kind of relationship. It could help lessen stigma and actually treat all citizens—single, in relationships or otherwise—with respect. Marriage's benefits, of stability, legal ease and economic pay offs can still be met, without institutionalisation.

All this shouldn't deter fights for things like gay marriage—indeed, that cause also is about undermining marriage assumptions and norms.

For myself, I can see no reason that sufficiently makes marriage, in general, a viable option worth wanting or supporting. I would much rather live in a society that had little interest in my relationship life, but protected me and everyone nevertheless. It's not a black-and-white situation of total societal interest or disinterest. Keep marriage, if you so want, but it shouldn't hamper or restrict others from benefits or equal treatment, especially when there appears so little reason for having it.

Periodical and Internet Sources Bibliography

The following articles have been selected to supplement the diverse views presented in this chapter.

Pooja Bedi, "Is Marriage a Dying Institution?" *Times of India*, March 12, 2017. https://timesofindia.indiatimes.com/blogs/heartchakra /is-marriage-a-dying-institution/

Anna Brown, "A Profile of Single Americans," Pew Research Center, August 20, 2020. https://www.pewsocialtrends.org/2020/08/20/a -profile-of-single-americans/

Christina Diane Campbell, "A Darker Side of Singlism: Discrimination in the Legal Code," *Pyschology Today*, May 31, 2020. https://www.psychologytoday.com/us/blog/living -single/202005/darker-side-singlism-discrimination-in-the-legal -code

Mandy Len Catron, "What You Lose When You Gain a Spouse," *The Atlantic*, July 2, 2019. https://www.theatlantic.com/family /archive/2019/07/case-against-marriage/591973/

The Economist, "The State of Marriage as an Institution," November 23, 2012. https://www.economist.com/special-report/2017/11/23 /the-state-of-marriage-as-an-institution

Edwin J. Feulner, "Marriage at Risk in America," Heritage Foundation, October 1, 2012. https://www.heritage.org/marriage -and-family/commentary/marriage-risk-america

Gaby Galvin, "US Marriage Rate Hits Historic Low," *US News and World Report*, April 29, 2020. https://www.usnews.com/news /healthiest-communities/articles/2020-04-29/us-marriage-rate -drops-to-record-low

Amber Lapp, "Working-class Christians and the Future of Marriage," Institute for Family Studies, October 12, 2020. https://ifstudies .org/blog/working-class-christians-and-the-future-of-marriage

Jan Fullerton Lemons, "Future of Marriage," CQ Press, December 1, 2017. https://library.cqpress.com/cqresearcher/document .php?id=cqresrre2017120100

New York Post, "The Future of Marriage," May 29, 2011. https:// nypost.com/2011/05/29/the-future-of-marriage/

Amisha Padnani, "Is Marriage a Prize?" *New York Times*, May 15, 2020. https://www.nytimes.com/2020/05/15/arts/women -marriage-pop-culture.html

Roni Caryn Rabin, "Put a Ring on It? Millennial Couples Are in No Hurry," *New York Times*, May 29, 2018. https://www.nytimes .com/2018/05/29/well/mind/millennials-love-marriage-sex -relationships-dating.html

Suzanne Venker, "The Future of Men and Marriage Is Bleak," *Washington Examiner*, June 14, 2019. https://www .washingtonexaminer.com/opinion/the-future-of-men-and -marriage-is-bleak

YourArticleLibrary, "The Future of the Institution of Marriage." Retrieved January 5, 2021. https://www.yourarticlelibrary.com /marriage/the-future-of-the-institution-of-marriage/31308

For Further Discussion

Chapter 1

1. Do you think marriage is an agreement between men and women? Why or why not?
2. What are the different aspects of marriage, and how do they all play into the institution of marriage?
3. Why do you think the marriage institution was created by humanity?

Chapter 2

1. What are some forms of marriage that the viewpoints in this resource did *not* discuss in detail?
2. Do you think economics or social aspect is more important to people when they marry?
3. How do you think the history of marriage influences modern-day ideas of marriage?

Chapter 3

1. What legitimate concerns and conflicts do some feminists have with the concept of marriage?
2. Do you feel same-sex marriage has always in some form been recognized? Did that change when religion changed?
3. Why do you think recognition of divorce is necessary in societies?

Chapter 4

1. Do you think the institution of marriage will survive?
2. Are arrangements such as living together or domestic partnerships as valid as legal marriage?
3. Do you think same-sex, interracial, polygamous, or open marriages will become more accepted in the future?

Organizations to Contact

The editors have compiled the following list of organizations concerned with the issues debated in this book. The descriptions are derived from materials provided by the organizations. All have publications or information available for interested readers. The list was compiled on the date of publication of the present volume; the information provided here may change. Be aware that many organizations take several weeks or longer to respond to inquiries, so allow as much time as possible.

American Association for Marriage and Family Therapy (AAMFT)

112 South Alfred Street
Suite 300
Alexandria, VA 22314
(703) 838-9808
email: central@aamft.org
website: aamft.org

The AAMFT is a professional organization dedicated to promotion of marriage and therapy worldwide. It was founded in 1942.

Center for Law and Social Policy

1200 18th Street NW
Suite 200
Washington, DC 20036
(202) 906-8000
website: http://www.clasp.org

CLASP is a national, nonpartisan, anti-poverty nonprofit advancing policy solutions for low-income people. Its focus is on developing practical yet visionary strategies for reducing poverty, promoting economic opportunity, and addressing barriers faced by people of color.

Smart Marriages: Coalition for Marriage, Family and Couples Education

5310 Belt Road NW
Washington, DC 20015-1961
(202) 362-3332
email: Diane@smartmarriages.com
website: www.smartmarriages.com

Smart Marriages is dedicated to making marriage education more widely available to the public. In addition, Smart Marriages supports community marriage education initiatives, legislation, and research.

The Dibble Institute

PO Box 7881
Berkeley, CA 94707-0881
(800) 695-7975
website: www.dibbleinstitute.org/

The Dibble Institute promotes relationship training for youth especially in the context of dating and romantic connections. Dibble's goal is to help young people build a foundation for healthy romantic relationships and lasting, positive family environments.

Girls Not Brides

65 Leadenhall Street
7th Floor
London EC3A 2AD
United Kingdom
email: info@GirlsNotBrides.org
website: www.girlsnotbrides.org/about-girls-not-brides/

Girls Not Brides is a global partnership of more than 1,300 civil society organizations from over 100 countries committed to ending child marriage and enabling girls to fulfill their potential.

Human Rights Campaign

1640 Rhode Island Avenue NW
Washington, DC 20036
(800) 777-4723
email: Membership@hrc.org
website: www.hrc.org

The Human Rights Campaign is the largest pro-LGBTQ organization in the US and was founded in 1980.

International Center for Research on Women (ICRW)

1120 20th Street NW
Suite 500 N
Washington, DC 20036
(202) 797-0007
website: www.icrw.org

ICRW is the world's premier research institute focused on tackling challenges facing women and girls worldwide, including, prominently, child marriage.

National Council on Family Relations (NCFR)

661 LaSalle Street, Suite 200
Saint Paul, MN 55114
(888) 781-9331
email: info@ncfr.org
website: www.ncfr.org

Founded in 1938, NCFR is the oldest nonprofit, nonpartisan professional organization focused on family research, practice, and education in the US. It is based in Minnesota.

National Marriage Project

University of Virginia
PO Box 400766
Charlottesville, VA 22904-4766
(434) 321-8601
email: marriage@virginia.edu
website: http://nationalmarriageproject.org

The National Marriage Project (NMP) is a nonpartisan, nonsectarian, and interdisciplinary initiative. The project's mission is to provide research and analysis on the health of marriage in America, to analyze the social and cultural forces shaping contemporary marriage, and to identify strategies to increase marital quality and stability.

National Organization for Marriage (NOM)

17 D Street SE #1
Washington, DC 20003
(888) 894-3604
email: contact@nationformarriage.org
website: www.nationformarriage.org

NOM is a conservative US nonprofit political organization established to work against same-sex marriage legalization. It was established in 2007.

Unchained at Last

108 Lenex Avenue #187
Westfield NJ 07090
(908) 481-HOPE
website: www.unchainedatlast.org
Unchained at Last is a nonprofit organization supporting the end of forced child marriage in the United States, providing crucial legal and social services to women, girls, and others.

Bibliography of Books

Cara Acred. *Marriage*. Cambridge, UK: Independence Educational Publishers, 2017.

Jana Marguerite Bennett. *Singleness and the Church: A New Theology of the Single Life*. New York, NY: Oxford University Press, 2017.

Kutter Callaway. *Breaking the Marriage Idol: Reconstructing Our Cultural and Spiritual Norms*. Downs Grove, IL: IVP Books, 2018.

Joanne Marie Ferraro. *A Cultural History of Marriage, Volumes 1-6*. New York, NY: Bloombury Academic, 2019.

Maurice Godelier. *The Metamorphoses of Kinship*, London, UK: Verso, 2012.

Shoshana Grossband. *The Marriage Motive: A Price Theory of Marriage: How Marriage Markets Affect Employment, Consumption and Savings*. New York, NY: Springer, 2016.

Nora Haenn. *Marriage After Migration: An Ethnography of Money, Romance, and Gender in Globalizing Mexico* (Issues of Globalization: Case Studies in Contemporary Anthropology). New York, NY: Oxford University Press, 2019.

Aneeka Ayanna Henderson. *Veil and Vow: Marriage Matters in Contemporary African American Culture*. Durham, NC: University of North Carolina Press, 2020.

Jeff Iorg. *Ministry in the New Marriage Culture*. Nashville, TN: B&H Books, 2015.

Tayari Jones. *An American Marriage*. Chapel Hill, NC: Algonquin Books, 2018.

Arnaud F. Lambert. *Anthropology of Marriage and the Family*. Dubuque, IA: Kendall Hunt Publishing, 2017.

George Monger. *Marriage Customs of the World: An Encyclopedia of Dating Customs and Wedding Traditions.* Santa Barbara, CA: ABC-CLIO, 2013.

Linda Stone and Diane E. King. *Kinship and Gender: An Introduction.* Philadelphia, PA: Routledge, 2018.

Rebecca Traister. *All the Single Ladies: Unmarried Women and the Rise of an Independent Nation.* New York, NY: Simon & Schuster, 2018.

William Tucker. *Marriage and Civilization: How Monogamy Made Us Human.* Washington, DC: Regnery Publishing, 2014.

Paul Valentine, Stephen Beckermand, and Catherine Ales, eds. *The Anthropology of Marriage in Lowland South America.* Gainesville, FL: University of Florida, 2017.

Carol Cronin Weisfeld, ed. *The Psychology of Marriage: An Evolutionary and Cross-Cultural View.* Washington, DC: Lexington Books, 2017.

Index